SOMERSET

Red Manor in the Quantocks.

GENERAL EDITORS

VISION OF ENGLAND

CLOUGH & AMABEL
WILLIAMS ELLIS

SOMERSET

SYLVIA TOWNSEND WARNER

DRAWINGS BY
R. KIRKLAND JAMIESON

PAUL ELEK

THIRTY-EIGHT HATTON GARDEN
LONDON

Published in 1949 by
Paul Elek Publishers Ltd
38 Hatton Garden, London E.C. 1.
Printed in the Netherlands
Typography and collection of photographs
by Sarah Clutton
Jacket and cover design by Kenneth Rowntree

TO STEVEN CLARK

Catalogue No 199/9

CONTENTS

Bath.

I

IN SOUTH-EAST
SOMERSET

At the start I must admit that I have never been able to decide whether Somerset is a flat county with a quantity of hills in it or a hilly county of which a great deal is as level as a pavement. Like a shot silk, it depends which way you look at it. Since I can't find a definition, I must begin with a general impression; that one cannot travel through Somerset without feeling that one is being handed on from one set of hills to another, and that each set of hills has its own physiognomy.

Somerset lies on a geological hotch-potch, and expresses this in its sky-line. The geological map, expressing this in its shade-card of strata, looks as if some one with a taste for bright colours had emptied out a rag-bag. The eastern end of the rag-bag is the most animated, bordered with olive-green of Oxford Clay and rust-colour of Cornbrash, with Oolite canary yellows and Lias browns and Triassic terra-cotta twining round the sky-blue Limestone and purple-grey Coal Measures of the Mendips. To the west of the county the rag-bag sobers down with the brown mass of Exmoor's Devonian and the lesser mass of the Quantocks, with a tawny streak of Permian running between them; but even so there is room in the corner for a patch of emerald Greensand. And in the centre of the map, tattering inland from the Bristol Channel, is a territory of whitish alluvium: the dullest colour in the geological map, and in the map of surface colourings the brightest. For this is the watery willow country where the obstinacy of rivers and the obstinacy of man, the rivers flooding and eroding, the men ditching, draining, and embanking, have between them made that level expanse which is what one thinks of under the name of Sedgemoor — though its divisions are named King's Sedgemoor, West Sedgemoor, Burnham Level, Brue Level, Huntspill Level, Tadham Moor, and much else. A man-made territory such as this, where every hundred acres has demanded planning and labour and control, retains a great deal of locality.

It is the moors and levels which give such definition to Somerset's variety of hills. The Mendips, the Quantocks, the Poldens, all have an air of rising which is quite inconsistent with the heights to which they really rise. From even such moderate elevations as Hamdon Hill or High Ham one has the sense of looking down as decisively as a churchtower gargoyle, and the outline of Brent Knoll seen from across the Brue Level is volcanically imposing.

But of all the hills of Somerset, Glastonbury Tor must be the one which has impressed itself on the greatest number of beholders. It is, actually, and not only because of its associations, a notable hill, and a great landmark, haunting the skyline of central Somerset. Glastonbury Tor is an *outlier:* an obstinate vestige of former high ground, the rest of which has been worn away. This has given it a rather elementary outline. Perhaps it is too symmetrical to be shapely; and though the tower on its summit appeals to the part of one's nature which likes a flag on the tip of a sand-castle, it is too patently in the middle, and converts the hill into a very large socket. There is a Here-I-am-ishness about Glastonbury Tor which can at times be exasperating; but when some accident of lighting or vista has re-made it as a Sacred Mount it stands up as reassuring as it did for the pilgrims to whom it meant that the end of their journey was in sight.

Glastonbury is in the Isle of Avalon, *Insula pomorum quae fortunata vocatur,* the Earthly Paradise of Britain, and the burial place of King Arthur, whose bones, of a kingly largeness, Giraldus Cambrensis saw in a tree-trunk coffin. By legend and in fact, Glastonbury is a place of ancient inhabitation and ancient civilisation, too. The things discovered during the excavation of the British lake village near by show a high level of prehistoric culture. The inhabitants reaped with

7

iron sickles, wove and spun, used the turning lathe, knew about mortising, wheel-making, and hanging doors, made coloured glass beads, leaden weights, and fine pottery. Their dice were marked from one to six, and they attended cock-fights. If this were to be a history of Somerset, Glastonbury would be the place to begin it (for that matter, it would be a pretty good place to begin a history of England, too). But it is to be that much more uncertain thing, a book about Somerset; and though it cannot resemble a guide-book, since I am constitutionally incapable of resembling a guide, an err-and-stray-book would be nearer my measure, I must not outrage convention by beginning in the middle of my subject. Even an err-and-stray-book should start somewhere near a county boundary.

There is another notable hill of Somerset in the south-east corner of the county, Cadbury Castle, of which Leland writes, spelling with agreable freedom: 'Camalatte, sum tyme a famose Town or Castelle. Much Gold, Sylver and Coper of the Romayne Coynes hath be found there yn Plowing; and lykewise in the Fieldes in the Rootes of this Hille, with many other antique Thinges. Ther was found in *hominum memoria* a Horse Shoe of Sylver at Camalate. The People can tell nothing ther, but they have hard say that Arture much resorted to Camalate.'

No one resorts here now. Trees have grown up within the fortifications of this earthen castle, and in autumn they brim over like an arrangement of gigantic dahlias. On Christmas Eve King Arthur's knights ride two by two through the wood. Sequestered in a landscape of small steep hills, any one of which might have been fortified by Modred as a rival castle, Cadbury is lovely whatever way you approach it; but the best view is from the churchyard of Sutton Montis. At Sutton Montis a dynasty of Burtons were parsons from 1573 to 1771. Their names are recorded on the outer wall of the chancel. The Anatomy of Melancholy was a kinsman of these Burtons, [1] and it would be natural to suppose that he came here and studied his

subject among 'the plain footsteps of an old decay'd Camp.' [2] Natural, but quite fallacious. The Anatomy was not a travelling man.

It is an easy transition from Leland to the carved bench-ends in North Cadbury Church. They are sixteenth century work, and include among the usual range of gryphons and allegories and other *antique Thinges* a labourer who seems to have walked straight out of the fields in the roots of this hill, and a young man playing a large wind instrument of the shawm kind whose attitude and countenance are expressively musical. He is totally absorbed in the difficulties and raptures of performance. Somerset churches are rich in caved bench-ends. The bench-ends at North Cadbury are especially fine, and can be comfortably studied, for the church — a very stately one — is full of light from its great windows. The manor house stands beside the church, and that too is stately, with a long formal front which at the church end of the building breaks into an architectural rumpti-iddity of narrow windows and bits patched on.

This rumpled, rising and falling, well-timbered stretch of south-east Somerset is bordered with views of the Wiltshire chalk. Its towns are Bruton, Wincanton, Frome, and Castle Cary. The minds of Victorian educationalists turned naturally to evergreens, and small contiguities of shade mark the outskirts of Bruton, where a grammar-school was endowed in 1519. Bruton has a celebrated pack-bridge, and views down alleys and under dark archways of gardens sloping to the river. Castle Cary, with nothing so striking to boast of, has, I think, a greater air of period and integrity. Yet angry passions can rage among the serenest sash-windows and hooded doorways, and in 1769 Castle Cary was tossed by dissensions about church-music — always a fruitful ground for dissensions. 'Nov. 12. I was disturbed this morning at Cary Church by the Singers. I sent my Clerk some time back to the Cary Singers, to desire that they would not sing the Responses in the Communion Service, which they complied with for several Sundays, but this morning after the

8

Cadbury Castle, from Sutton Montis churchyard.

first Commandment they had the Impudence to sing the Response, and therefore I spoke to them out of my desk, to say and not sing.' 'Nov. 26. I read Prayers and Preached this morning at C. Cary Church. N.B. No singing this morning, the Singers not being at Church, they being highly affronted with me.' 'Dec. 17. The Singers at Cary did not please me this afternoon by singing the 12 Psalm, New Version, reflecting upon some People.'[3] Reflecting, in fact, upon Parson Woodforde of the Diary, then a young man and living at Ansford near by.

The fact that there is a spire at Castle Cary reminds me to say that Somerset, like Norfolk, is a tower county. There are various correct ways of classifying the Somerset towers: the pattern of their windowing, whether they are finished off with pinnacles or with an edging, etc.; and almost as many varieties of Somerset tower, or so it has seemed to me trying to observe these classifications. When I desist from trying it seems to me that So-

merset church towers are of two kinds: towers that go straight up, and look doctrinal, and towers with a spread, which look defensible. Evercreech, north of Bruton, is one of the celebrated Somerset towers, of the doctrinal variety. Those who find it rather too much so can console themselves with an admirable monkey (it is on the north wall) and go on to Batcombe, through a very pretty village called Westcombe, by lanes which in summer are fringed with cranesbill. Batcombe declares itself by the top of a tower appearing over the top of a hedge. After this stimulating introduction (even in such broken country it is unusual to meet the summit of a tower before you have set eyes on the rest of it) a re-adjustment of level swings Batcombe into its true figure — a square-headed tower of heroic girth and proportion, with the hillside rising behind it and falling below it. The interior of the church, with a lofty western arch to remind one of the tower, has a large wall tablet recording many members of the

9

Bisse family in a lettering which is like a dialect in its clumsy grace. The Philip Bisse, sturdily at prayer in a little brass in the chancel, is one of Fuller's Worthies. 'Extracted from a worshipful family in this county,' he left his library to the Somerset foundation of Wadham College.

The beauty of English villages is so proverbial that we take it for granted, and continue to admire villages where all the beauty has mouldered into the village slum or been mislaid among teashopped cottages and too many and too rambling roses. But Nunney is really a beautiful village, unaffectedly old, with a tranquil church-clock, and little footbridges over a little stream; and the ruins of its castle — 'a small but neat castle, built by the de la Mares, and hence called Nonney de la Mare'[4] — look more protecting than warlike. Nunney should again be called de la Mare, for it is exactly as if the poet had written it. The loveliest stanza in the poem is the house beside the castle. Its haunting air of being a lost princess goes far beyond the fact that its ground-floor windows repeat the pattern of the garden-front at Brympton d'Evercy. So much might be copied; but only a stylist could have established the grand-mannered fenestration in the modestly proportioned façade by those swinging roof-lines. Nunney Castle is protected as an Ancient Monument. I wish protection could extend to this house. The window-tax in the past has robbed it of some of its windows, and the twentieth century has fastened far too many wires to it.

Nunney is at the easternmost tip of the Mendips, and bellows of blasting from the local quarries break its quiet. The streams of this neighbourhood, being full of lime, were supposed to give a particularly good temper to steel. Nunney used to make edged tools, and making scythe blades was an industry at Mells, near by. Mells is an example of the Jack of All Trades history of this region of Somerset, so rich above and below ground, and as full of fortunate conjunctions as though Defoe had designed it. In quarrying country and on the edge of a coal-field,

Mells looks out on fields where the scythes were busy. It had an ironworks, too. But its chief business was cloth-making. It had its own plantations of woad for dyeing, and the fuller's earth for the tucking-mills needed only to be fetched from the country round Wellow and English Combe, villages a few miles to the northward. All this was wealthy wool-country once. Both Defoe and Cobbett had axes to grind, and ground them for opposite sides of the tree; but even allowing for this it is sobering to turn from Defoe's Frome 'which is so prodigiously increased within these last twenty or thirty years, that they have built a new church, and so many new streets of houses, and those houses so full of inhabitants ... that if their trade continues to increase for a few years more, it is likely to be one of the greatest and wealthiest inland towns in England,' to Cobbett's Frome, 'where I saw between two and three hundred weavers cracking stones, moving earth, and doing all sorts of work, towards making a fine road' ... unemployed, in fact, and starving.

Mells, for all its Jack-of-all-trades history, is likely to be recalled by most people because of a piece of specialisation — one of those steadfast English families who love the smoke of their own chimneys and become, as one says, 'part of the place they live in.' The Horner chapel in Mells parish church is dominated by Munning's equestrian statue of Edward Horner, who was killed in the first world war. Raymond Asquith, killed in the same war, is commemorated by an inscription cut by Eric Gill. This is incised in the actual stone-work of the tower wall, a feat of craftsmanship.

Just as we preen ourselves on beautiful villages we preen ourselves on old inns; and often as questionably. But there can be no doubt about The George at Norton St. Philip. When the Horners established themselves at Mells, The George had already comforted many generations of travellers. It was built in mid-thirteenth century as a lodging-house-cum-grange for the Carthusian house at Hinton near by. The George is

Mells.

not only very old and very grand — a three story building, and lofty at that; it is in extraordinary good preservation. If houses can be built under a lucky star, The George is certainly one of them. Passing from monks to merchants, for Norton St. Philip was a centre of the wool trade, a market and a fair town, it became an out-of-the-way old place just when prosperity would have rebuilt it or pulled it down. Its lucky star still prevails, for it is now respectfully and unaffectedly well-cared-for.

Monmouth was here in 1685, with all his malign stars beginning to blaze upon him. His room on the first floor, disused except for a few pieces of contemporary furniture, has a reproachful austerity. One wants to kindle a fire in the stone fire-place to comfort the ghost of that hapless profuse young man who brought so many good West of England people to misery, slavery, and

death. Their ghosts, too, might be heard snoring and tumbling in the great attic overhead, except that foot-ghosts seem to be exempted from walking. This attic, which runs from end to end of the house, is the greatest glory of The George. It is like a homespun banqueting-room.

Three summers after Monmouth was here so unhappily Mr and Mrs Pepys and Deb. arrived 'with great pleasure, being now come into Somersetshire' (Mrs Pepys and Deb. were both natives of the county). In this happy exploring frame of mind (signally so, for the day begins in Wiltshire with: 'Up, finding our beds good, but lousy; which made us merry') they had no sooner crossed the county border than they talked to little boys to hear the dialect, and in Norton St. Philip church saw 'the tombstone whereon there were only two heads cut, which, the story goes, and credibly, were two sisters, called the Fair Maids of Foscott, that had two bodies upward and one belly, and there lie buried.' This, of course, was delightful, and the bells were 'mighty tuneable',[5] and the dinner was good (it cost 10s for a party of five) ; and so they went on to Bath.

II
BATH

Some towns are indifferent to the quarters of the compass. Approach them as you please they will turn you much the same face — usually rather a dull one. Others, like Edwardian beauties, have a right or a left profile. One of the pleasures of becoming on intimate terms with such towns (as perhaps with Edwardian beauties) is the discovery of the charms of an uncelebrated aspect. But this is all geography and masonry. History has a word to say also. A wind out of the past rustles the pages of the guide-book, and if one is to arrive properly one must have that wind behind one. Bath lies at the end of a westward journey, and is attained by the London-Bath road.

'If you leave me to suggest our destination, I say Bath.' It was Mr. Pickwick who said it, adding, as a reason in keeping with the aims of the Pickwick Club, 'I think none of us have been there.'

This seems a shocking admission for a reputable grown-up English gentleman with a taste for travelling. But when Mr. Pickwick spoke Bath was falling into its nineteenth century sleep. Cheltenham was more fashionable, foreign cures 'were beginning to supersede English spas, and the healing Art was moving away from anything so mild as 'taking the waters' in favour of Lady Southdown's Black Draught and Mr Carlyle's Blue Pills. Deeply as one must compassionate the victims of Victorian medicine, those who endured the penitential nastiness of its tonics, the awful fervour of its pills and purges, one has to be thankful that during the Victorian age Bath was out of fashion. It would not look as it does, otherwise. The Pump Room, for instance, would have been re-modelled to resemble the waiting-room of a gothic railway-station (so much more in keeping with the Abbey opposite) ; a large and Lombardic hospital in yellow and blue brick would have broken the monotony of Royal Crescent; the Assembly Rooms would have been pulled down (thus sharing the fate of nineteen of Wren's City churches) long before Goering sent out German bombing-planes by Baedecker; and as the century ripened a dismal flounce of something like Bournemouth would have draped the environs. Thanks to calomel, and later, ozone, these improving touches fell elsewhere. Bath remained an eighteenth century town, and towards the close of the century became more of a Roman one; for it was in 1878 that the City Corporation set their architect, Major Davis, to excavate Aquae Sulis systematically.

The Romans travelled to Aquae Sulis by Pontes (which is the river crossing at Staines) and Calleva Atrebatum (which is Silchester) if they came from the southern half of Britain; or through Corinium Dubonorum (which is Cirencester) if they came from the north. Either way, at the close of their journey they passed beneath the hill and British stronghold of Solsbury. Sul of the hill and the hot springs in the valley below was a British deity before she became the goddess Sul-Minerva. The Roman was kindly disposed towards deities; he accepted them wherever he found them and (almost as though he were a Scotsman) traced cousinships with deities of his own. Minerva, an armoured goddess, was a patron of medicine too : she could be comfortably cousined to a British goddess presiding over a healing spring and a fortressed hill-top.

Sul, a British Goddess, is the hostess of Bath. The first recorded bathers are, of course, Prince Bladud's pigs. Seeing them look so much the better for their wallow Bladud wallowed too, and was cured of his leprosy. Then, being a proper prince of Britain once more, he built a city and a temple, and finally fastened winged shoes to his feet and jumped off the temple roof in an endeavour to fly by Art-Magic. Bladud is a very fine early specimen of the English eccentric, and I daresay he closely resembled Walter Savage Landor.

The pigs bathed. In all probability the Britons bathed. They were heathen, and the heathen are usually given to bathing. Then came the Romans, and made a Roman city. Aquae Sulis was in essentials very much like a later Bath: there were the Thermae, and Sul-Minerva's temple, and a forum, and a few houses, some of which I suppose let lodgings. The Roman habit of inscribing on stone, which makes them so comfortable to antiquarians, allows us to know some of the people who visited Bath, or died there: a town councillor, a sculptor, soldiers of the Sixth and the Twentieth Legions. Other visitors came from Northern Gaul, and no doubt the overseers of the lead mines in the Mendips came to Aquae Sulis for a little relaxation and to do some shopping. The great bath, by the way, is floored with Mendip lead of Roman making.

It is melancholy to think of the last days of Aquae Sulis, and of the backward glances which must have been cast at the kind, safe city, and of the valetudinarian regrets of those who knew they had bathed for the last time in those 'three hot springs, of a blewish & sea-colour, which exhales a thin sort of mist, and something of an ill-savour'.[6] As for Sul, she went back to her dower house hill, for a Christian country had no use for her. Good stone blocks, however, are always useful. Though the Saxons made havoc of Bath, a monastic foundation settled in the ruins, and was a well-established Benedictine house by Domesday Book. In 1090 John de Villula, Bishop of Wells, moved his see to Bath, 'which occasioned some hot disputes between the Monks of Bath and the canons of Well'[7] — disputes now peacefully interred in the double title of the see. Six centuries of grass must have laid a good stout wadding over the Roman baths by this time, though the memory of the healing spring

still persisted; in the 12th century Bishop Reginald founded a hospital (we should call it a hostel: the hospital of the Middle Ages succoured the sick but did not undertake to cure them) for poor people who came to use the waters.

It is unlikely that Bath had more than a hole-and-corner sort of reputation during the Middle Ages. Its hot springs were never baptised into Christianity, no saint took charge of them. Possibly Sul on her hill was too near a neighbour. The western church was chary of poking up old local deities. [8]

I said that travellers along the Bath road travel westward. There is one notable exception. I cannot see the Wife of Bath travelling any way but eastward. The morning sun shines on her broad face under her flapping broadbrimmed hat, and brightens her scarlet hose and her business-like spurs as she sets out on one of her jaunts.

> *Thries hadde she been at Ierusalem,*
> *She hadde passed many a straunge strem,*
> *At Rome she hadde been, and at Boloigne,*
> *At Galice at Seint Jame, and at Coloigne.*
> *She koude muchel of wandrynge by the*
> *weye.*

And no doubt she was well acquainted with The George at Norton St. Philip, which is a very agreeable reflection.

The Wife of Bath represents Bath during those centuries when it was a place where people lived, rather than where people visited. Looms clacked, church bells rang, the Guild of Weavers held its feasts and its acrimonious committee meetings. An error on the part of time which I bitterly deplore is that the Wife of Bath was dead before Bishop King enriched the front of Bath Abbey with the sculptures of Jacob's Ladder. I am sure she would particularly have enjoyed the angels head-downwards.

Trade was not so brisk in the seventeenth century, and Bath had grown 'a verrie little poore cittie' when antiquarianism became fashionable and Bath a place to visit. Evelyn came here during that tour when he showed his young wife the beauties of England. He bathed, though Mrs Evelyn did not. Thirty-four years later Pepys was: 'up at four o' clock, being by appointment called to the Cross Bath, where we were carried one after another. And by and by much company came; very fine ladies; and the manner pretty enough, only methinks it cannot be clean to go so many bodies together in the same water. Strange to see how hot the water is; and in some places, though this is the most temperate bath, the springs so hot as the feet not able to endure. But strange to see, when men and women herein, that live all the season in these waters, that cannot but be parboiled, and look like creatures of the bath! I staying above two hours in the water, home to bed, sweating for an hour; and by and by comes musick to play to me, extraordinarily good as ever I heard in London almost, or anywhere. 5s.' [9]

A Fellow of the Royal Society and a buyer of new books, Pepys no doubt had read the *Account of the Bath Waters* in the *History of the Worthies of England: endeavoured by Thomas Fuller. D.D.*

Having explained that the waters contained *Bitumen, Niter,* and *Sulphur,* Fuller continues:

'But how these waters come by their great heat, is rather *controverted* than *concluded* among the Learned. Some impute it to Wind, or Airy Exhalations, included in the Bowels of the Earth, which by their agitation and attrition (upon Rocks and narrow passages) gather Heat, and impart it to the waters.

Others ascribe it to the heat of the sun, whose Beams, piercing through the pores of the Earth, warm the Waters, and therefore anciently were called Aquae Solis, because both dedicated to, and made by the Sun.

Others attribute it to Quicklime, which we see doth readily heat any water cast upon it, and kindleth any combustible substance put therein.

Others referre it to a Subterreanean Fire, kindled in the Bowels of the Earth, and actually burning upon *Sulphur* and *Bitumen*.

Others impute the heat (which is not *desstructive,* but *generative,* joyned with moisture) to the fermentation of several Minerals.'

After all this, the wary Fuller contents himself by remarking: 'The worst I wish these Waters is, that they were handsomely roof'd over.'

Gentlemen have never been more handsomely roofed than at this period, and it is pleasant to imagine the chestnut, the black, and the golden periwigs shining against the grey stone, parties of elegant visitors strolling through the narrow streets, climbing the green hillsides, eating chicken and kissing girls. But there was a boorish and raffish element too, which hung about Bath to pick up what it could at cock-fights and card-tables. 'Splenetic, rustic, and vulgar' — so Goldsmith described the company at pre-Augustan Bath. It took a genius in manners, a genius in architecture, and a philanthropist, to make Bath beautiful, distinguished, and respectable (though even then Wesley must needs call it 'the head-quarters of Satan'). The genius in manners was Beau Nash. Nash had come to Bath to make his living as a gambler, but with a gambler's daring staked his career on the turn of the wheel which had brought politeness and urbanity uppermost. Himself neither polite nor urbane, he became Bath's Arbiter of Elegance. He abolished boots from the Pump Room. He put down the wearing of swords and spurs. He chastised the Englishwoman's assumption that anything will do to wear in the country. He enforced cleanliness, early hours, orderly behaviour. He got the streets paved and lighted. He combated rowdy *sederunts* in taverns by building Assembly Rooms where people could game on light refreshments. At the same time he kept every one well amused, and attracted more and more persons of distinction. When the Abbey bells rang for the arrival of some notable visitor the company left card-tables, medicinal sipping, conversation, and divine service (Nash, however, had made going to church part of the fashionable routine) to run out and see who had come now. Never had Satan's headquarters been more civilly organised, and a proof of this is the fact that Selina, Countess of Huntingdon, that evangelical Semi-

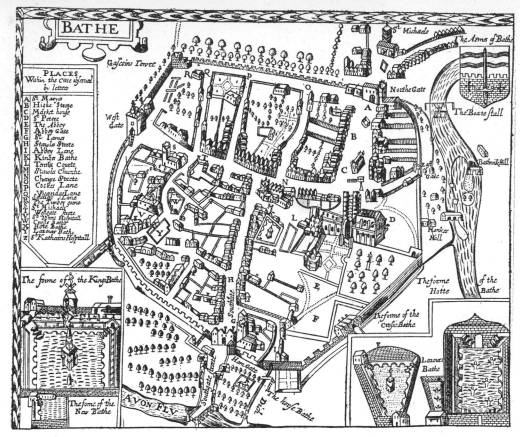

Map of Pre-Georgian Bath.

ramis, and one of Satan's most ardent adversaries, lived in Bath herself.

So much for the genius in manners. The philanthropist was Ralph Allen, who did good by stealth and gave two hundred guineas to Fielding. He came to Bath as a post office clerk, devised and carried out his own postal system, grew rich, bought the Combe Down Quarries, and set himself to convert Bath into a city which in politeness and urbanity of building should match the politeness and urbanity of Beau Nash's society. The project was practical — but I really cannot think it was less philanthropic for that.

'The ashlar back-yards of Bath' — so Thomas Hardy asserted — 'have more dignity than any brick front in Europe.' I suppose this is partly an expression of the architect's feeling about stone; and certainly Bath's back-yards are very dignified, and some streets and squares of fallen fortunes near the railway had a sombre majesty beyond even Dublin's Belisarius slums. [10] But the stone-built dignity of Bath is compounded with many of the qualities one associates with the best style of brick: qualities of moderation and sobriety and — one might almost say — prudence. When you recover from the excitement aroused by the longitudinal magnificence of Wood junior's Royal Crescent or the sweep of Wood senior's Circus you realise

15

that the unit on which the whole is built up is a dwelling-house, a dwelling house whose dimensions are stately, but still human. Bath is a conversational city: when the situation justifies it, as in the two great Crescents, the conversation rises to eloquence — but never to rhetoric. The contribution of a third architect, Robert Adam's Pulteney Bridge, is like a summary of Bath's grand-mannered conversational style. The arches, making their nobly proportioned sentence about the River Avon, carry a street of small shops across it.

It is Allen and the first Wood we have to thank for the design of Bath, from the Parades which border the river to the streets and terraces which make the hillside as positive as a façade. Uniformity of building material, conformity of style, have much to do with this effect. But there is a quality in the lay-out of Georgian Bath which is more often found in the elevation of one great building than in the arrangement of a town.

As one looks at this architectural hillside it becomes peopled with names in the Dictionary of National Biography just as the west front of Wells Cathedral is peopled with names from holy writ. There is Queen Square, where Miss Austen liked the lodgings 'with dirty quilts and everything comfortable' (I pause to disagree with editors who suggest *dimity* as an alternative reading to *dirty*) and hoped that the Duchess of York's removal would make the price of salmon more reasonable. There is New King Street, where William Herschel discovered the planet Uranus (in his spare time, for he was a professional musician). There is the Circus, where Gainsborough set up his easel. There is Gay Street, with Fanny Burney on one side of it and Mrs Piozzi on the other, there is Rivers Street where Prince Bladud Savage Landor expressed his individualism by liking Bath in mid-nineteenth century, and up there in Lansdown Crescent the old Beckford, a smoky beacon, ended his days. That is one way of looking at this view. In another mood it resembles an interior wall of Bath Abbey, a mosaic of moderately distinguished, unselfquestioning good society. When I have been inside Bath Abbey for a minute or two I become aware of a sort of well-bred English mumble going on all round me. Heavens, what quantities of people are here! It is ridiculous to look about for celebrities, no doubt they abound, but then there are so many others, who to themselves are just as well worth celebrating: for here is an Admiral, and here is a Divine, and there a Member of the Privy Council, and there a Gentleman eminent for Unaffected Piety, and there the Daughter of an Earl. And here, almost under my right foot, is *Evan Lloyd, of Pengwerne, Esq.;* and in that compact assertion what a mountain of Welsh pedigrees!

When one has admired the façade of Bath from below one should climb those steep streets and consider Bath from above. Trees emerge like fountains, roofs coalesce and slide downhill, the river crooks itself round the peninsula. There is the Abbey, and the pavement in front of it where the pigeons strut with so much deportment, and the Pump Room, the Roman Baths, the hot springs. There, rimmed by the solemn Roman masonry, in the water that reflects the sky and one's contemporary face as one leans over, is the eye of Bath... a green eye; for the 'blewish and sea-coloured' water leaves an orange stain, and these tints between them make up a smouldering lime-green. The three springs pour out half a million gallons a day. Their volume has never been known to alter, their temperatures never vary. They are radio-active. It is probable that they rise from a depth in the earth's crust not less than 5,000 feet. It is a queer experience to look into the well-shaft of the Hot Spring. As the heavy metal doors swing open one sees a pit in the rock, and a rising steam moistens one's face and fills one's nostrils with the odour that was old and mysterious long before a Roman nose snuffed it. This steam, rising with such gentle drowsy force, makes the stone-built city seem ephemeral. The Roman masonry, the old city walls, the Georgian town, the stone terraces rising one above another, are no more than the concentric petals of a rose. The sculptor from Cirencester, the ravaging

Pulteney Bridge.

Saxon King, the long line of Abbots and Bishops, the Georgian notabilities, the innumerable people who have come here in search of health, of entertainment, of history, of husbands ('I had a small property, and I went to Bath. Several of my friends had found charming husbands at Bath. However, time slipped away, madam, and by some strange fatality or other, I exhausted my little resources, and did not manage to get settled in life: that is the truth of it')[11]... the steam obliterates our outlines, we all look pretty much the same, and none much anterior to another.

Priddy.

III

THE MENDIPS
GLASTONBURY
AND WELLS

'In climbing a hill Mrs Chamberlayne is very capital; I could with difficulty keep pace with her — and so we posted away under a fine hot sun, stopping for nothing, crossing the Church Yard at Weston with as much expedition as if we were afraid of being buried alive.' Weston is on the way to the celebrated view from Stoke Brow, and Mrs Chamberlayne and Miss Jane Austen were out walking to enjoy a prospect. 'A fine

extensive prospect' — the words come naturally to one's lips in the country round Bath, where the hills are so shapely and the slopes so green and the vistas between them as blue as dinner-plates, and the trees so well-grown and well-grouped. There are architectural prospects too: Prior Park, with its Adam Orangery, and Shockerwick, and Kelston (though I wish the original Kelston Manor were still standing, because Sir John Harington built it and lived there with his *rare dogge* Bungay, and loved it with all the enthusiasm of his nature. One must hanker for the home of this extravagant fantastic creature, who had more than a dash of Montaigne about him, and translated Ariosto, and invented water-closets, and got Bath Abbey re-roofed by the expedient of taking the Bishop there on a wet day and engaging him in conversation under a drip). The landscape round Bath is like a handsome and well-groomed horse. As for the valley of the Avon, to go through it on some October morning when the first frost has set fire to the woods and the meadows have their second flush of green, and then to find Bath sunning itself round the corner is like going from a Mozart adagio to a Mozart minuet.

Travelling from Bath to Wells one skirts the coal-measure country round Radstock and Midsomer Norton; and because of the animation of railway bridges and viaducts, and the slag-heaps, so oddly classical, and the heavily charged shades of green which develop from coal being underneath, the landscape becomes more scenic, dashed with opera and Salvator Rosa. Grocer's shops have plate-glass windows, public-houses stand boldly on corner sites, and there are a great many more dogs than can be accounted for by the greater density of human population, for dogs are an industrial phenomenon. So are whited doorsteps and window-sills, and polished brass knobs. So is not the magnificently ornate tower of Leigh upon Mendip. Though this is not a large coal-field it has the true coalfield air of being slightly defiant and separatist — a world of its own, like opera, and, like opera, with a higher incidence of sudden

Burrington Combe.

death.[12] The grandest scene, though, of this landscape, is a little further north, at Pensford, where the railway viaduct goes over the village. For a piece of rhetoric, this would be hard to beat. Camerton, near Radstock, was the parish of the Reverend John Skinner — as much an *Enfant du Siècle* as de Musset, melancholy, thin-skinned, cantankerous, as voluminous as Coleridge, accumulating his slag-heap of diaries, and consoling himself for the England of the post-Industrial-Revolution period by digging for British and Roman remains.

With the smell of the slag-heaps still in the back of one's nose one comes on Farringdon Gurney, where there is a remarkably handsome house. Standing at the junction of two dull main roads, it is as arresting as a Dryden couplet in a newspaper article.

Further on, and much easier to miss, is the Wolf of Rome. It stands on the roof of Mendip and at the road-side. But though this is the latest of the Roman remains in Somerset — indeed, it is perfectly contemporary — it has contrived to sink into the locality. This is its story, as it was told me. An Italian prisoner who was working for a local farmer, was set to build a wall along the road. When the wall was completed the prisoner, who perhaps had come to love the place where he had been working, the wide view and the comb of trees, asked if he might build a monument on the wall in memory of his wife, who had been killed in an air-raid. The permission was given, and the monument was constructed, a tall slender arch carrying the Capitoline Wolf, the one with the very small Romulus and Remus. They sit comfortably under her belly with head-room to spare. She shelters them with an air of universal dispassionate maternity, and turns her heavy head to look over Mendip. There will be many more imposing monuments of this war, and many (alas! perhaps) more durable than this slender arch. But I doubt if any will be more interesting.

Soon after the Wolf of Rome the road begins to pour itself downhill, and one descends to the Christian side of the Mendips. I don't mean this invidiously. But one cannot cross such a great bulk of stone without having a sense of frontier; and looking down on central Somerset the first thing one sees is Glastonbury Tor sailing on the flats like Noah's Ark; and so I repeat, the Christian side of the Mendips.

Joseph of Arimathea came to Glastonbury with his staff, his gospel, and his companions, travelling by boat through the reeds and the thickets of the fen, and landed at Glastonbury, in the isle of Avalon. He had been advised in a dream to look for a hill resembling Mount Tabor; and here it was. He thrust in his staff, and it took root, and blossomed on the day of Christ's nativity. He wove a small chapel out of reeds and osiers, and this was the beginning of the Abbey. He preached his gospel, and founded Christianity in Britain. That is one story. Another attaches Glastonbury to Saint Collen, who fought Gwyn ap Nud, a prince of darkness, on the summit of Glastonbury Tor, and overcame him (all Satans like high places and haunt them: like Mrs Chamberlayne, they are very capital in climbing a hill). Whoever founded Glastonbury, it is undoubtedly very old, and perhaps the first site of Christendom in our island. It was a place of holy burial, and claimed to have sepulchred not only King Arthur, Saint Dunstan, and three Saxon kings, but a great number of saints: among them Saint Patrick, Saint David, Saint Aidan, Saint Teiso, with remains and relics of saints from foreign parts, including three of the Holy Innocents. This might seem no more than part of that 'huge system of monastic lying, in which Glastonbury has a bad pre-eminence.' But

there is rather more to it than that. Gwyn ap Nud was a prince of the underworld. Glast and Avallac were also gods of the dead, and the isle of Avalon is where Morgan le Fay carried Arthur: 'for I will into the vale of Avilion, to heal me of my grievous wound. And if thou hear never more of me, pray for my soul.' This Avalon was a pre-christian paradise, like the green kingdoms under a hill where Tamalin and Thomas of Erceldoune were conveyed by the faery; and whether Joseph or Collen founded Glastonbury, they built their beehive huts and sang their hymns and husked their corn in a place that was hallowed by an earlier reverence, like swallows plastering their colony on an old barn.

The thought of this double antiquity, the beginning of our antiquity laid in the lap of a further antiquity yet, endears Glastonbury in the mind. Perhaps it might be better to leave it there, and go no further. It has been given a red-brick suburb of incomparable nastiness, and its industries are lodged in factories of no distinction. Within these environs is a smallish town with a great deal of traffic going through it, a handsome church, some old house-fronts, a pilgrim's inn which might be a match for The George at Norton St Philip, but its neighbours squeeze it, and the remains of Glastonbury Abbey in a green-grassed enclosure. They are very beautiful (except for the kitchen, which is sturdy, but not, I think, beautiful), and very well-kept. The grass is well-kept too, no grass could be greener or smoother. Visitors who come here remark with one accord that it is wonderfully peaceful. And so it is. It is almost impossible to conjure up the vivacity and energy of a great mediaeval Abbey in surroundings so respectfully calm. Nothing is amiss, but my ungrateful heart assures me that something has gone wrong, just as something has gone wrong at Old Sarum. Sometimes I have thought that a clue might be found in a passage of a guide-book. 'In 1906 the site of the ruins and the adjoining estate were offered for sale and a public subscription was inaugurated to secure so precious a relic for

A farm on the Mendips.

the National Church... To celebrate the acquisition a Thanksgiving Service, attended by King George V and Queen Mary, then Prince and Princess of Wales, and many leading prelates and clergy, was held on June 22nd, 1909.'[13] It would take one a long time to get over anything like that, especially if one were already old and infirm.

To be given the mitre of Bath and Wells automatically hoists a clergyman of the Church of England into popularity. Be he never so austere a moralist or never so fierce about the diocesan finances, he cannot be mentioned by his title without arousing feelings of affection; for the Bishop of Bath and Wells, like Leda, is irrevocably associated with swans. There must be a number of people who, if asked what they knew about the Bishop of Bath and Wells, would reply, 'He feeds the swans when they ring their bell.' This picture of a Bishop seated in his palace garden with a little bread-basket beside him, ever ready to spring up and feed his bell-ringing swans, is so totally erroneous that I hope it may be immortal. Just now the bell-ringing is in abeyance, because of our national economies; but I expect the swans keep a religious remembrance of it, and meanwhile they seem to be doing pretty well, both by the kindness of disorderly people like myself who throw things in, and by what they dredge by their own industry from the bottom of the moat (I was delighted to realise, the last time I was in Wells, that a swan reversed, that is to say with his foreparts under water and his croup in the air, presents very exactly the outline of a mitre). Where in the world is there a pleasanter strolling-place than the leafy walks that accompany the moat that surrounds the walls that encompass the palace of the Bishop of Bath and Wells? The moat is so broad that it reflects the quivering wall and the treetops rising above it. At one corner there is an inrush of water, a constant liquid voice and stir. Along one wall are espaliered old fruit-trees, and some delightful peonies.

21

Above the wall one sees trees waving, the ruins of the old banqueting house, built in a convivial rosy stone, and the grey towers of the cathedral.

There is a draw-bridge, too; a fact as well-known as the swans. I myself had known it for years, but never fully till the day when I saw a furniture remover's van draw up, and removing-men begin to carry furniture across the draw-bridge. Though reason assured me that really there was no other method of moving-in a bishop of Bath and Wells, something higher than reason riveted me to the spot; and presently my mind's eye was watching a procession of enthralling richness and variety. Over the draw-bridge went iron-bound coffers, mahogany dining-tables, cradles, wine-coolers, lutes, grand-pianos and spinets, lecterns, roasting-jacks, dutch-ovens, prie-dieus, ottomans, buffets and tall-boys, four-poster beds and truckle-beds, jardinières, sewing-machines, marble pastry-boards, statues of saints and statues of heathen deities, books past counting from Crockfords to *Incunabuli*, reliquaries, baro-meters, iron cauldrons, coffee-urns, hour-glasses, umbrella-stands and wig-stands, robes lined with fox-skins, perambulators, iron safes, and coffins. All this time the furniture of the current bishop was passing before me and when the men had finished with their load they climbed into the van and went away. But in my mind's eye the procession over the draw-bridge continued, and gradu-ally the furniture gave place to bishops: great bishops, small bishops, lean bishops, brawny bishops, brown bishops, black bishops (attending a pan-Anglican congress, no doubt), grey bishops, tawny bishops, grave old plod-ders, gay young friskers ... There is a great deal that is fascinating in the Church of England, and I don't know a quieter place to study it in than Wells.

Wells is the gentlest of all our cathedrals. There is not a frown in its architecture. Even the St Andrew's Cross expedient which sup-ports the central tower, though it expresses a moment of architectural desperation, (for it was put there when the weight of the tower was beginning to crack the foundations), has a good-hearted Blunderbore candour about it, as though some mild local giant had come in to lend his shoulders. Wells owes much of its serenity to the good manners of Bishop Jocelyn, who completed the nave as it had been begun under an earlier bishop in-stead of branching out into better ideas of his own. He preserved the continuity of the nave and built the West Front. It is as openheartedly beautiful as a hedge-rose and, if one can eventually leave off admiring it, confronts one with the usual problem of west fronts: whether the entrance should conform to the scale of the building or to the scale of the worshipper. The doors at Wells look like three mouseholes in a skirting.

Show-beauties, like the Wells chapter-house, are not really any less beautiful for being notorious, though sometimes one has to scheme a little to get them in the right light. The cathedral has plenty of unsung beauties too; that seventeenth century lectern, for in-stance, full of the majestic mildness of Eng-lish Baroque (a matter of workmanship, I think; one can see the same combination of mildness and majesty in a good English-made boot); and the cope chest, which looks as though it contained some strange instrument of music, and is a very haunted piece of fur-niture. I do not mean haunted in any spec-tacular sense; but it exhales a spirit of usage which is impressive.

It is a thousand pities that we are so often forced by circumstances to have only a slot-hole view of the places we visit ... lands where it is almost always afternoon. I suppose any sensible person visiting Wells would know that he must stay till sun-down. But if he goes away after seeing the centre tower imparadised by the glow of sunset, he goes much too soon: the Falling-Asleep of the Blessed West Front which follows is quite as beautiful; and only then, I think, does one realise how satisfactorily the cathedral is tied to its surroundings by the line of buildings on either side. Then, too, the cats come out — the fortunate cats in residence, fortunate as vicars-choral — and pace with dignity on the

22

From Priddy by the Ebbor Rocks.

darkened sward. Later on, doors open, and restrained voices call them in. Even then it is not too late—on a spring evening—to enjoy the Vicars' Close, where rays of greenish gaslight give a doubled sense of retirement from the world. Somebody may be playing the 'cello; and there are still birds mixing music and shrieks in the Deanery garden. The eastern aspect of the cathedral, with all its complications of choir and chapter-house and lady-chapel, keeps resolving itself as one walks on, like the progress of a Tallis motet. If one looks over the other shoulder one discovers house after house, nobly built, richly ornamented, all with that particular air of leisure which makes the Georgian house so engaging. (Quite fallacious, no doubt. It is a useful check to architectural Cranfordism to people such houses with the bawling, squalling, bullying family of Miss Clarissa Harlowe). But even when one has called up half a dozen black-hearted Canons, whose children defy them, whose dinners disagree with them, whose summer evenings are ravaged by money troubles or religious doubts, one's senses continue to assure one that nobody could really be totally unhappy in Wells.

If Wells rewards a keeping of unusual hours, Cheddar Gorge demands it — or else you must go there at some unvisiting time of year. Early on a summer morning it is romantic landscape in perfection. One seems to be looking at it over Richard Wilson's shoulder — its shadows are so deeply shadowy, its contours so dramatic, its lighting so expressive. One stands in a well of shadow and rocky cold; and overhead, perched like birds on the face of the cliff, small trees and bushes glitter with dew. It is so silent that presently it is not silent any longer. One has begun to hear a muted intermittent tick-tock of dropping water. It is somewhere in this cleft of the rock; or in this; or it comes from that overhanging mass that has the tree on it. Then one realises that it is as much everywhere as grasshoppers are. For it is the voice of limestone, and this noise of an

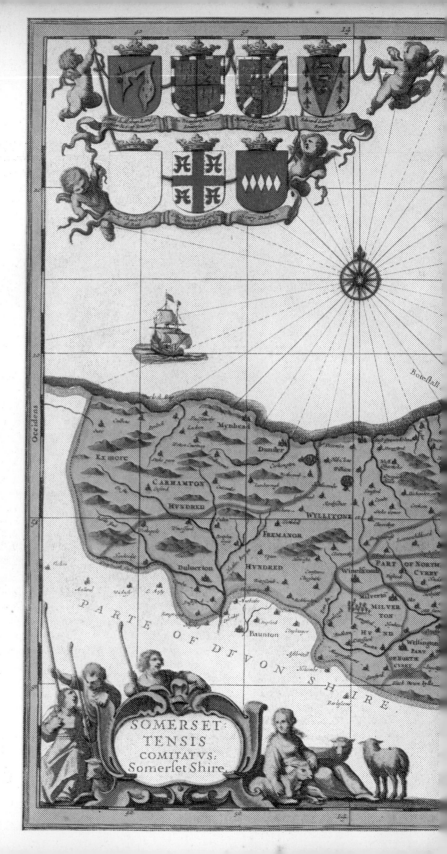

Map of Somerset, published by Valk and Schenk, 1683. (Originally engraved by John Janson, and first published in 1646). Lent by P. J. Radford, Fareham.

PARt OT GLOCES-
TER SHIRE

Parshut Point

PORTBVRI
HVND

BROCKLEY
HVND   HARTCLIFE &
BED MINSTER
HVND

WINTERSTOAKE
PART
HVND

Ashridge

Mendip Hills

WELLES

BRISTOLL

KEYNSHAM
Cateiham
CHEWI   Peniford

HVND

CHEWTON HVND

WELFORD

Gedney more

BATHFORM

BATHE

HVNDRED

WELLO
HVND

HVND

FROME

KILEMERSDON

HVND

HART

Steit Poynt

GANING
NORTH
PETHERTON

Brent Marshe

Brent marsh

WHITELEIGH

Heth more

Andie
Island
Glasembury

WELLES   HVND

HVND

HVNDRED

GLASTON HVND

WHITTON
Stepton Mallet

BRVTON

HVND
Bruton

WILT

HVND
SEDGO

Sedeg more

Denes more
HVNDRED
Andre More

SOMERTON
SOMERTON

HVND

HVND

NORTON FERRIS

HVND

HVND

HVND

PITNEY

PVLTONE
HVND

Langort

KINGSBVRI
HVND

MARTOCK HVNDRED

Martock

Ibchefter

STONE
HVNDRED

HVNDRED

HORN
HVND

HVND

HVND

CHEW

COKER

SHIRE

Amfteloslami
Apud G. Valk et P. Schenk

PART
OF DEVON SH:

Oriens

Milliaris Anglica

intermittent tick-tock is sounding throughout the bulk of the Mendips, and far beyond human reckoning is constructing stalactites and stalagmites that no one will ever see.

Other stalactites and stalagmites have been seen repeatedly, ever since the day in 1837 when Cox's Cave was accidentally discovered by an inn-keeper who was poking about for a place where he could build a coach-house. *L'homme propose.* Round the outside of the Cheddar Caves there are booths selling post-cards and souvenirs, tea-shops, Teas and Minerals, car-parks; but as far as I can see, no coach-house. Summer charabancs arrive. The very idea of a coach-house is ridiculous. Yet sometimes the most ephemeral and fortuitous ghosts are the best at haunting, and the inn-keeper who wanted a coach-house and got a Delphic cavern instead has a foolish wistful immortality of frustration. Meanwhile the Cheddar stream rushes out through a cleft in the rock, and is timeless and conscienceless as all running water is.

The road through the Cheddar Gorge sweeps upward from right to left, into the sun and out of it, and brings one out in Derbyshire, somewhere between Matlock and Buxton. Roads with grassy margins run between dry-stone walls. Bare bright fields extend on either side, and a long way off a solitary house has wrapped a few trees round itself against the wind. Even the map, saying *Miners' Arms* and *Castle of Comfort Inn*[14] puts on a Derbyshire accent; and Nordrach, another name on the map here, has a singularly back-of-beyond resonance. This is the Mendip of the old lead mines. The Ordnance Map of Roman Britain shows a road running to Charterhouse on Mendip, where the lead mines were worked by the Romans and perhaps by the Phoenicians too. One says *worked;* but probably the word should be understood as having gone through the change from quantity to quality, from working oneself to profiting by the work of others; for I suppose the miners themselves were mostly native islanders.

When a trade is sufficiently dangerous, like mining or seafishing, it becomes a sort of state within the state, and has its own laws and jurisprudence. 'The oulde auncyent custum of the occupasyon of the myneris in and upon the Quyns maiestis forest of Mendip' (a Marian record of customs and traditions which had been accumulating during earlier centuries) has one clause which is very expressive of such professional autarchy. 'Item and if therebe any man by thys doutful and dangerous occupasyon tack hys deth and ys slayne by faulyng of the yerth upon hym, by drownynge, by styffling with fyer or wother wyse as in times past meny hath ben so murthryd the coroner nother no officer of the Quyns majestys hath not to do with the boddy nother with hys or there goods but the myners of that occupasyon shaulle fetch up that ded boddy, out of the yerth at their owne proper costs and chargs and also to burye hym in Chrystyn buryall allthough he do tacke hys deth 1x faddum under the yerth as herby sore meny a man so hath ben lost.'

These words, so stern and melancholy and stand-offish, are part of the tune of the wind that blows down the old gullys and sings through the dry-stone walls. There is an *Avaunt to Coroners* look about this great bulk of limestone lifted out of the rest of the county. The contours of limestone are always severe, it has none of the rounded obstinacy of chalk. Chalk yields in dips and scallops. The resistance of limestone is full of breaks and warfares, dips are sharpened into hollows, valleys into gorges. The rock is always on the alert. You see the rock-face look out from behind a clump of waving grasses, and it is as alarming as though a lion had reared up and looked out at you. As for the old lead workings, time has muffled them but it has not smoothed them. Under a wadding of grass and fern the ground lies in a resentful disarray.

Cheddar Gorge is only one of the several clefts that wind into the flanks of this great scrolling plateau. Burrington Combe on the eastern side is impressive almost as it were by force of logic. It zig-zags through a narrow defile between steeply inclined slants of rock, and every turn of the road repeats the same

The Miners' Arms.

austere pattern of triangles, the same rather harsh colouring and absence of rhetoric. If I were a superstitious person I think I might be considerably alarmed by the sober formidability of Burrington Combe where, if there should happen to be an Apollyon straddling right across the way, he would argue me down with the precision of an Aquinas.

Whichever way one climbs to this plateau of the Mendips, there is the same impression of being very high up and in a locality that keeps itself to itself. It is a landscape without surprises. The scattered farms stand up to the eye, you see them from a long way off, they are plain and unambiguous, with a straight track leading to them, and their outbuildings round them and the line of washing prancing in the wind. It is a landscape without fears. The scattered tree-clumps are tall and well-grown, nothing looks sickly or sinister. And yet there is something rather formidable about the place: 'a wildish destiny.' Its solitude is so positive, so much a matter of fact. This matter of fact wildishness

characterises the village of Priddy. Priddy is a loosely-knit village of small stone houses held together by a common relationship to a large green with a quantity of small roads going off from it. One has the feeling that however the course of history might have gone on down below, Priddy would have been just what it is.

If you walk on past the inn and an avenue of trees, seeming all the nobler for being there for no apparent reason, you come to the edge of Mendip and look out over the most startling view in Somerset — a sickle-shaped view sweeping from the Wiltshire downs to the mountains in Wales and containing all the central level to the line of the Quantocks. Everything is there, towers, towns, villages, roads and rivers, woods and orchards and Sedgemoor's banks of green willow, and the wall of the Mendips crumbling into the Bristol Channel and reappearing in the two islands, Steep Holm and Flat Holm, a final assertion of the tonality of limestone, like the final chords of a symphony. Every-

27

thing is there, even a collier going up the Bristol Channel from the port of Cardiff to the port of Bristol. Then, if you are a Priddy man, you turn your back on this and return to Priddy.

When I heard the guide in Wookey Hole say that the river Axe rises under Priddy I felt that I was not the only person to feel the impact of Priddy's personality, and that if I had been inclined to make too much of it, I was not alone in my weakness. The river Axe, said the guide, speaking categorically and with a weight of learned opinion behind him, rises under Priddy.

Beyond the innermost of the visitable caves at Wookey three more have been attained by exploring divers. Beyond these must be others, and others again. They may be lofty or cramped, gothic in their fretted ornamentation or classically severe. They may be white, or yellow, or red-ochre-coloured. But they are in darkness. The river may flow quietly, or force its way through narrow gulleys, or leap down chasms. But it is unheard. Divers have carried an electric light into the first of these further caves. The guide turns out the other lights and switches this one on. Standing in darkness one sees illuminated water flowing under the low lintel of the rock. It is the river Axe, beginning under Priddy and visible at last.

The water is so perfectly transparent that the bed of the stream seems within reach of one's hand, though really one would have to dive to it. [15] Except when a drop of water falls into it from the rock overhead and is answered by a momentary flash of silver like a minnow leaping, the surface of the stream is smooth as a mirror. There is only one word for its movement. It glides.

One falls into a solemn thoughtfulness watching this underground river, which is so transparent, so speechless, that it is like a disembodiment of water, and so like the Styx that it even has a flat-bottomed boat on its stone shore. It is even more like the Styx when the people being shown round by the guide obediently descend the slope and stand by its brim. English sight-seers are notably

mild, and at first it is natural to suppose that people visiting Wookey Hole feel awed by their surroundings; but presently one notices that they look oddly at home there, as if some atavistic affection for caves had settled them in. Two successive races of paleolithic man used these caverns, living in an odd domesticity with hyaenas. 'The latter cave-haunting animals were the normal occupants, driven out of their dens when the nomad hunters encamped there and kindled their fires for cooking. Their visits were sufficiently long to allow of the accumulation of chips knocked off in the process. When the thin line of smoke disappeared, and the ashes of the fires were cold, the hyaenas returned to the cave and ate up the remains of the animals left by the hunters.' [16] While I was thinking of this, and reflecting on the hyaena-like satisfaction with which I myself eat up the cold scraps after my visitors have gone away, and on the enormous span of time comprised in these caverns hollowed by water and then filled to the roof by dung and debris left by prehistoric men and animals, and on the stealthy drop by drop longevity of a stalactite, and deciding that anything so fleeting as man has no scope to do more than to be at home wherever he finds himself, the guide, who had been talking of the river's variations in volume, pointed to a high-water mark on a bank of sand. A voice said 'How did that sand get in here? Who brought it?' It might have been the voice of the British Constitution — it was so dutifully and profoundly suspicious of an encroachment. The guide answered that the river had brought the sand along; and everyone looked relieved to hear it. For though the growth of a stalactite expresses an enormous slowness, grow it does; and man, seemingly so fleeting, grows too, and develops himself in abstract shapes of duty and integrity, and is ready to resent sand being brought into the Wookey Hole.

The river Axe, which has known no light except artificial light, comes out into the light of day at the foot of a cliff, and immediately begins to glitter and babble and trots off to be industrious among some quarrying-sheds.

Mendip Cottages.

Thence it flows along the base of the Mendips, past Axbridge, which is a handsome small town of great antiquity (it was a Saxon Borough) with a proudly situated church approached by a long flight of steps, and ends between Bleadon Hill and Brean Down with all the pomp of a ferry.

IV

INLAND FROM THE SEVERN SEA

It is one of the pleasures of map-reading when the sea invades the map and the nomenclature of hill and valley goes under water. The Bristol Channel has nothing quite so endearing as Thames-Mouth's Mouse, and Knock-John, but it has Culver Sands (Culver means dove, and I wish some one would tell me if it were the pattern of shoal-water which recalled the irridescence on a dove's neck), and English Grounds and Welsh Grounds and Usk Patch — water-marks as familiar to sailors and fishermen as the landmark of the Shiplett Firs, on the ridge of Bleadon Hill, which they call 'See Me, See Me not.'

As seas go, the Bristol Channel is a recent creation. The Severn made it, and the west wind, bringing rain from the Atlantic to break on the Welsh mountains and hurry down brooks and streams and rivers into the great marsh between England and Wales. In this debatable ground the to-and-fro of tide and river washed round headlands and subdued them (there is a drowned forest near the coast-line at Porlock), broke limestone rock into pebbles and swirled the pebbles into solid beaches, pulled and swept and silted and pounded until the channel was made. It is a precarious balance. In 1548 the people of Yatton in the North Marsh were fighting against 'the rage of the salt water' and applying for the stone of their old chapel to build into a sluice. There was another great

sea flood in the seventeenth century, and Defoe in his *Tour* tells how 'this low part of the country, between Bridgwater and Bristol, suffered exceedingly in the terrible inundation of the sea, which was occasioned by the violence of the wind in the Great Storm, anno 1703, and the country people have set up marks upon their houses and trees, with this note upon them: "Thus high the waters came in the great storm:" "Thus far the great tide flowed up in the last violent tempest," and the like. And in one place they showed us, where a ship was, by the force of the water, and the rage of the tempest, driven up upon the shore, several hundred yards from the ordinary high water mark, and was left in that surprising condition upon dry land.'

The Ordnance map draws no boundary line to show where the Bristol Channel becomes the River Severn, but it indicates that this change takes place near where the prehistoric fort of Worlebury Hill rears morosely above the amenities of Weston super Mare. It is obvious that a great many people must like Weston super Mare, since a great many people go to it. It is functionally one of those places that number only sunny hours, and the hours of sunshine at Weston super Mare are published daily during the holiday season and do it credit; but I would like to put in a word for its winter aspect, when the chairs are folded away, and curtains begin to be drawn against the early dusk, and the sea has the beach to itself and lounges to and fro, rustling like a be-wintered tortoiseshell butterfly. I am astonished that the English melancholy which led our grand-parents to take so much pleasure among ruins does not send more of us to enjoy the seasonal ruin of holiday resorts. And the ambiguity of the Severn Sea, whose seaward half is insisted on by the full titles of both Weston and its neighbour, Burnham, gives a particular poetry to their winter Limbo aspect. It was beyond the Worlebury boundary, at Clevedon (where Coleridge and Sara hung their Æolian harp in their cottage window)that T. E. Brown wrote:

Lime works at Cheddar.

The sea was Lazarus, all day
At Dives gate he lay,
And lapped the crumbs.
Night comes;
The beggar dies —
Forthwith the Channel, coast to coast,
Is Abraham's bosom; and the beggar lies
A lovely ghost.

It is the dark quarter of the moon for Brown's reputation. He is, I'm afraid, a very mongrelly poet; for he bounds and gambols at the wrong moments, his feelings are exuberantly sensitive, and the words he brings in and makes idols of are only too often (like that deplorable *forthwith*) fetched straight from the garbage-heap. But mongrels have their days, and I think Brown had one of his when he saw that the tidal water of the Severn Sea was Lazarus. All the apparatus of the sea is here: it moves, it smells salt, it has waves and gulls and sand-dunes,

just as all the apparatus of the man was in the beggar, but thwarted by sores and circumstances and being laid at Dives gate. The Bristol Channel is a deprived kind of sea, sallow and dispirited; but with the power of becoming a lovely ghost.

Though the Clevedon of *In Memoriam* has suffered a seaside change, Tennyson could still walk over the fenny level of Nailsea Moor and Kenn Moor and find it looking like a Lincolnshire landscape, even to having a spire in it. Congresbury is one of the rare Somerset spires, and very beautiful it looks, and very elegiac. Yatton, on the further side of the lesser Yeo[1], has a tower which gives the impression of having tried to make the best of both worlds, being topped with a sort of truncated cone, like a spire cut off at the knees. This gives it a crazy Wren-ish appearance, as though that inventive genius had sketched it out after dining with some men. Yatton church has a singularly beautiful porch, and a tall church-yard cross, and is neighboured by an ambiguous old house which ought to have the ghost of an antiquarian in it, still planning to throw in some gothic touches.

One can be a long time in this marginal country without thinking of Bristol (though there might be a hint of it in the way that Yatton is strung out along the road, for most Somerset villages are built compactly). By Wraxall, where there is another fine church-yard cross, and with the rising of Leigh Down, there is a perceptible hybridisation of of city and country: wooded properties, and mansions nestling, and some bungalows which do not nestle at all, being of the date when it is more healthy to be wind-swept. But the Gordano valley, lying between Leigh Down and Portishead Down, keeps a great deal of character in its narrow privacy, and has several good things in it: the descent into Clapton in Gordano, for instance, with the pale Severn brimming up the middle distance, the remnants of the old Clapton in Gordano manor house, and Weston in Gordano church. This is out of the run of Somerset churches, for it is small and sober. Ecclesiologists delight in it because its porch contains a rare survival: a Palm Sunday platform above the church door on which choir singers stood in a row to greet the entering procession. Naturalists might delight in it too, because of the carved bird in the Chancel. It is a water-bird, a shag, I think; and there are two versions of it, a *cantoris* and a *decani* shag, carved in relief by some one with a masterly sense of design and as much inwardness as Bewick.

Easton in Gordano has an epitaph which combines a prevalent local last line with a previous line so succinct that it is difficult to accredit it to the date on the stone—which is 1858.

In love he liv'd in water he died
Life was desired but God denied.

And there you are, left to make what you can of it. My own view of it is that he was drowned in the Avonmouth docks. Since I am stumbling over graves, Clapton in Gordano has a fine narrative epitaph.

Both stout & strong was I
In Plymouth Hospital to die
I did escape the raging seas
And so at Plymouth end my days
At nineteen years my doom I met
Strange the sun in the morning set
Sudden the small pox seized me
And terminated all my misery.

Five years after the small pox seized the sailor Miss Hannah More retired from London life to a cottage at Cowslip Green; which is on the Bristol-Bridgwater road between Broadfield Down and the Mendips (a road which has some of the best motoring miles in Somerset where it sweeps round the tip of the Mendips). Hannah More's sun was considerably more advanced than the sailor's— she was forty—and her intentions were the usual placid intentions of those who settle down in the country. 'I am become a perfect outlaw from all civil society and orderly life,' she wrote to Horace Walpole. 'I spend almost my whole time in my little garden ... employed in raising dejected pinks and reforming disorderly honeysuckles.' Two years later she was busy with sterner varieties of dejection and disorder. She had noticed — it often happens to amiable intellectuals who retire to Cowslip Greens—the condition of her neighbours. [18]

Hannah More is now a classical example of Pie in the Sky philanthropy. But in fairness one should remember that though she expounded, she did not invent it. Philanthropy raged at that date, just as the smallpox did, and both were fostered by the same social conditions. Smallpox seized the sailor, philanthropy boiled in the veins of Hannah More. It was the same infection, though differently expressed. If one reads, not the *Annals of the Charitable Labours on Mendip*, but Hannah More's own letters one finds that she set out with a respectable womanly wish to meddle and mend, and some quite good notions about soup and filthy lucre. 'I find that spinning linen is a starving employment: a woman must add great skill to great industry to get one shilling and sixpence per week; whereas the same exertions will enable her to

OPPOSITE Glastonbury Tor.

SVMERSETE.

2. A page of Somerset Manors from Domesday Book (the apparent erasures are really underlinings).

Picture Post

3. The Alfred Jewel.
Ashmolean Museum

4. The Glastonbury Bowl. *Desmond Laing*

5. The castle of the de la Mares at Nunney: a fourteenth century hybrid of castle and dwelling house, it is more chivalrous than warlike.　　*E.S.B. Elcome*

6. The dovecote was an important feature in manor-house economy. This is at Norton St Philip.　　*F. R. Winstone*

7. Nunney Manor House, c. 1700.　　*Country Life*

9. The remains of Hinton Priory, one of the two Carthusian houses in Somerset. The dovecot was in the upper storey - a roof of murmuring sound above the Carthusian silence. *Leonard & Marjorie Gayton*

8. The mediaeval packhorse bridge at Bruton; wide enough for a horse, and the parapet low enough for the overlap of a wool-pack.
Crown Copyright

10. 'The George' at Norton St Philip. A worthy temple for the patron saint of England. *Leonard & Marjorie Gayton*

11. English architects have composed many love-songs to Italy — none lovelier than Wood Senior's Palladian Bridge at Prior Park.

National Buildings Record

LEFT CENTRE

12. Royal Crescent, built by Wood Junior in 1769. 'What's one and one and one and one and one?' the White Queen asked. It depends who puts them together. *B. & N. Westwood*

14. Carving from the temple of Sul-Minerva at Bath. This may be by a British artist, working under Roman influence; and certainly it is a British countenance. *Spa Committee*

13. The Roman Circular Bath. The stone is worn away by dawdling Romans. *Humphrey & Vera Joe*

15. 'The ashlar back-yards of Bath.' Moor-fields Place. *National Buildings Record*

RIGHT CENTRE
17. Bath keeps many of its original shop-fronts. These, with no airs about them, but very graceful, are near the Abbey.
Reece Winstone

16. The grapes of Bacchus, the shafts of Eros, the snakes of Aesculapius.... detail of a frieze in the Circus.
B. & N. Westwood

18. Pulteney Bridge, by Robert Adam, 1770. Bath is a nobly timbered city - witness the limes in Queen Square. Pulteney Bridge is the lovelier for its tree.
Leonard & Marjorie Gayton

19. Low Ham. The mosaic pavement of a Roman villa, with scenes from the story of Dido and Aeneas. *S. Brown*

OPPOSITE
21. Looking down into Cheddar Gorge.
Fox Photos

20. Fragments of a 'pig' of lead, mined at Charterhouse-on-Mendip under the Romans. *Somerset Archaeological Society*

ABOVE AND BELOW

22.-23. Wells Cathedral. The Resurrection Tier.

Phillips' City Studio

LEFT

24. Wells Cathedral. The Lectern. 'This Brazen Deske' was given by Dean Creighton in 1669 'upon his returne from fifteene years Exile with his Soveraigne Lord Kinge Charles ye 2'. *Philips' City Studio*

OPPOSITE

25. The choir stonework of Wells Cathedral seems to become more and more rarefied as it escapes from the bulk of the tower, until it finally puts on the celestial body of the great east window. *Crown Copyright*

26. Wells. The wall and moat of the Bishop's Palace.   *A. F. Kersting*

27. The roof timbers of the Abbot's Barn at Glastonbury.   *B. & N. Westwood*

28. The tower of Dundry Church was paid for by the Merchant Adventurers of Bristol. It is a notable seamark. *Reece Winstone*

30. Cider-making on a farm. The apples are being passed up to the loft, where they will go into the cider-press. *The Times*

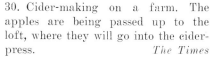

29. Mrs Hannah More, in the church porch at Wrington. It is interesting to compare this late Georgian bust with the Sul-Minerva head. No 14.

Reece Winstone

31. The railway viaduct at Pensford.   *E. W. Tattersall*

32. A corn-mill, an apple orchard, and the river Yeo, at Congresbury. *Mustograph*

33. At Pill the last hillside slopes down to the Gordano flats, and the Avon flows on towards the Severn through a landscape averaging 24 feet above sea-level.   *Fox Photos.*

34. 'Mr Holloway's flock.'   *Edwin Smith*

35. Bridgwater: house-fronts along the river Parret. Most of them are ugly, and they rub elbows with no regard for planning; but in the river they are all romantic, and all going to sea. *Crown Copyright*

36. A traditional Somerset industry. Harvesting teasels — used in surfacing woollen cloth. *The Times*

get near three shillings by spinning wool. Now it strikes me that it would be both pleasant and profitable if they could be taught...' and on she goes with her scheme. This was written in 1789; but written, alas! to Wilberforce, who was as much Hannah More's undoing as Faust was Gretchen's.

Hurrying from Shipton to Cheddar, from Nailsea to Yatton, climbing to those villages on Mendip 'considered so ferocious that no constable would venture there,' the ghost of Hannah More haunts this neighbourhood, distributing great quantities of bibles, but also buns. Hedonists at any rate should have a good word for her. For though the bibles may not have done much to improve the living conditions of those who received them (and for that matter the effect of the buns was only temporary) it seems indisputable that the hymns and the flutter and the funerals (above all, the funerals: 'the undertaker from Bristol wept like a child, and confessed, that without emolument, it was worth going a hundred miles to see such a sight') gave pleasure to people who badly needed it.

Hannah More's bust, with a wonderful cap, guards one side of the church door at Wrington, and on the other side of the door is John Locke, who was born there. The busts were originally designed as garden statues, and are very life-like and animated—so much so that one is driven to wonder what they talk about during the long evenings. Neither of them could stomach an atheist, but such a subject must soon be exhausted. This Wrington porch seems as sociable as Bath Abbey, for all the mural tablets inside the church were transferred here as part of a renovation in 1860, though that cleansing gale failed to uproot a remarkably grisly little flagstone inlaid with a white marble hand which points to the vault of a local family.[19] It must show the littleness of my mind that I recall this detail along with so many other things better worth remembering: the western arch (grand western arches are a feature of Somerset churches, complemental to grand towers), the architectural elegance of the device by which the narrow mouldings which compartment the

nave wall are carried up to encompass the clerestory windows in a cusped frame, and the frankness of the hand-book to the church, which tells visitors what to regret as well as what to admire. Hannah More is buried here, and so is a teddy-bear, which I found interred, with trust and piety, if not altogether efficiently, in a nook of a north wall buttress.

Among the more statutory zoology of the church is a magnificent lion who canopies a niche on the chancel wall. There are some more nice animals among the gargoyles of Burrington church near by. These are cited in Cox and Ford's *Parish Churches of England*, and certainly the *Frère Jehan* personage with the wine jar is superlative, though for a general level of gargoylish grandiosity I think I would give the palm to Mudford in southeast Somerset.

Skinner, writing in 1832, growls that Blagdon's beautiful tower 'has been degraded by a modern nave... the most ugly and ill-proportioned of any I have seen in these times of Church disfigurement.' Blagdon should have been a beautiful village, for its situation under the wooded slope of the Mendips is ravishing; but some wicked fairy must have come to the christening with a gift of benevolent marplots, for it is peppered with bad buildings of good intentions. The church had a thirteenth century carved screen, and got rid of it in some frenzy of improvement. The screen was put away in a farm house at Aldwick, and later was offered to Blagdon again. Blagdon refused it, and now it is at Butcombe, a small dusky church among the foothills of Broadfield Down. One has to wait a little and develop owl's eyes before one can see it properly, but it is worth waiting for. It is worth pausing, too, to look at Butcombe church from the further side of the narrow valley, whence it has a great air of being in the background of a Bellini altar-piece.

Further to the east, under Dundry Hill, is the river Chew, flowing past the village of Chew Magna, where Locke's friend Strachey lived at Sutton Court 'eating crammed capons and apple pies'—a thing I would not be averse to doing myself in such pleasant apple-pie scenery. At Stanton Drew, a little further along the river, is a Druidical stone circle. Whether or no one agrees with Dr. Johnson that when a man has seen one druidical temple he has seen enough, Stonehenge conditions most of our minds as to druidical backgrounds; and the Stanton Drew stones seem queerly placed in their mild pastoral landscape. But one should not pin too much faith to the mildness of landscapes. Dundry is said to have the finest hill pasturage in all England, but more than flocks have been watched there. From Dundry Hill you could see, night after night, Bristol bombed and blazing, brightest of all on that night of deepest frost, when the Elizabethan conceit of 'I burn in ice, in fire I freeze,' came so terribly to reality.

Miserere from Worle.

V

CÔTE D'OR : THE SOUTHERN BORDER

For the hundred people who travel with eyes there are perhaps thirty who travel with ears, and remember among the events of a journey the ring of a forge, the mock-turtle sobs of a draining-pump, the Sunday burst of hymnody (so much like the gush of juice when one cuts open a rhubarb tart) from church or chapel. As for travelling with a nose, that is rarer still . . . except of course for those ungrateful noses which quiver only for bad smells. The geology which gives Somerset such a variety of hills gives it a variety of smells too. I blame myself that I have not given an account of them. But there is one, at least, which must not be passed over: the smell of the apple.

There is no season of the year when the smell of the apple is out of Somerset. In winter it puffs from cottage chimneys. The midsummer sun brings an echo of burning apple-wood from the wood of the growing tree. The smell of cider floats from doorways, the smell of cider passes you on the road as the labourer goes by. But this is no more than the first orchestral evocations of the choral hymn in the Ninth Symphony: the real thing begins in August with the first windfalls. The apples are heaped in mounds under their trees, and lie there, sucked by wasps, and cooked by September noon-days. A persuasive tipsiness fills the air—though if you go too near these apple mounds the persuasion changes to something more like a blow on the head. This is the time of year to choose some moonlight night and walk through a landscape of black and silver snuffing up the rich pagan smell of apples, giving out the warmth they have gathered all day long—and to wish that Keats had come to Somerset for the cider-harvest. He would have liked the nomenclature, too: pomace is a most Keatsian word; and Cap of Liberty, Redstreak, Monday Apple, Kingston Black, Dabinet, Royal Wildings, Court of Wick Pippin, are words ready to drop into a poem's lap. Cider is still home-made in many Somerset homes, and homestead orchards have their special apples, nameless mossy old trees. The celebrated Redstreak apple, which a Parliamentary Commission in 1896 regretfully reported as extinct, may well linger in one of these little orchards, anonymous but still cherished for its power to make cider 'racy, poignant, oily, spicy.' These are the qualities which good cider should have, and which commercial cider too often hasn't; for the type called *Sweet* is not poignant, and the type called **Dry** is not oily. But things may improve. The National Fruit and Cider Institute at Long

50

Ashton is doing a great deal to restore the right tradition, and makes very good cider itself. [20]

Except for Exmoor there are few places in Somerset where one can't see an orchard: farm orchards, where the branches of one tree tangle with those of another, modern plantations with the trees running in tidy perspectives, roadside strips, hillside patches, or apple fields set down among fields of potatoes and fields of hay. On Sedgemoor it is pretty to see orchards moated with a wide ditch and walled with pollard willows. One does not realise till one has been among orchards in spring how many variations of tint the pink and white of apple-blossom can achieve. And one misses a great deal of pleasure if one only attends to orchards during the season of bloom or bearing. The crackle-pattern of winter apple-trees is charming, especially in old orchards where the trees have been allowed to develop their eccentricities.

If space were allowed me to develop my own eccentricities I could say a great deal more about apples. But I must come out of these orchards, and turn to brambles. Somerset is uncommonly rich in brambles. 'The best bramble ground may be found along the ridge of Blackdown and near Chard,' says the Rev. H. C. Binstead, writing in the *Victoria County History of Somerset*. Indeed, I remember to this day a morning spent in a very dewy upland pasture near Chard where the blackberries and the button mushrooms were alike in such a state of excellence that I ate them by turn and felt, as nearly as a human being can, I daresay, the solemn wet-footed contentment of a cow.

Then there are the Mosses. 'The wealth of Somerset mosses may be judged by the fact that during his short residence in Wells' (we are still with Mr Binstead) 'he found, within an easy walk of that city no less than 160 kinds of mosses.' This fact I had dimly apprehended as a likelihood myself. But if I had the mixture of energy and contemplation required for distinguishing 160 kinds of mosses I would like to undertake a survey of yet another thing in which Somerset is extremely wealthy: the middling dwelling-house.

The Somerset house has an English physiognomy: perhaps that is a polite way of saying that it has no very striking features. It has a broad open countenance, its door is in the middle and there is a pair of windows on either side of the door. These windows are apt to be, for the date of the house, old-fashioned: casement windows with rather heavy stone mullions. This appearance of 17th cent. windows in 18th cent. houses gives a pleasant feeling of rurality. The same type of window in the upper storey is set close under the line of the roof. Roof lines are usually level, though houses of more pretension may have a small pediment. Dormers are not common, gables are rare, and so are breaks in the line of the frontage. Somerset middling houses, in fact, are the houses of builders, rather than the houses of architects or individualistic owners; but they are houses built by very good builders, and in an excellent tradition. Above all, they have the beauty of being built of very good stone.

Ham Stone, Bath Stone, and Doulting Stone, are the predominant stones. But there are many lesser-known quarries that give a particular accent of colour or surface. Wedmore, for instance, is full of a local limestone, and at Bishop's Lydeard there is an almost plum-coloured sandstone which is perfectly delightful. Stone and skill both being indigenous, the middling Somerset house is liberally served in such matters as gate-posts, hoods to doorways, and little gazebos perched on the angle of garden walls.

Stone nowhere shows to greater advantage than in barns; and though the architecture of barns is so classical that it can hardly be said to vary from county to county, I can't think of Somerset without remembering Preston Plunknett, near Yeovil, where a farm court-yard, with a fine old house, has one of the loveliest barns imaginable.[21] Then there are the old cloth-mills and factories. Some of these are very handsome in a severe Quakerish way; and not always unornamented, for the mill-bell may be housed under an elegant

51

little cupola that has the graces of a curlicue billhead above a business letter. Wool seems to warm piety. In the 15th century the wool-staplers built church towers, and in the late 18th century the weavers built chapels. These have not lasted so well, but there are still a few of them, and their fragile classicality seems as pure as a pitch pipe—the more so when one remembers the braying ostentation of later specimens. One of the books waiting to be written is a book on Chapel Architecture. But I am supposed to be writing about Somerset, and at this juncture I should be addressing myself to the southern border of the county: the *Côte d'Or* one might call it—for the Ham Hill quarries colour it.

It is iron which gives Ham Hill stone its tawny colouring. The quarrymen bicycling home at the end of their day go past like bumble-bees, gilded with a stone pollen, and the village of Montacute, lying under its sharp name-hill, is all the colours of a honeycomb. Montacute is an old place, with a great deal of pride and character. It calls the open space in the centre of the village *The Borough,* and over shop windows the names of the proprietors are cut in the stone itself—a stately detail. There was a Cluniac monastery here. Its gate-house is part of Abbey Farm, and its dove-cot stands in the farm meadow. But the glory of Montacute is Montacute House, an Elizabethan House *pur sang,* built all of Ham stone, with the Nine Worthies ranged along the third story of its east front. Montacute, like Mells, is a house of long ownership. Edward Phelips built it, and Phelipses lived here for three hundred and fifty years. But I daresay there are constancies of as long standing among lesser local families, for this neighbourhood seems to evoke a peculiar love in those who live in it. Leland tells how the Montacute monks, having fallen on bad days, 'were compellid to beg for a certain season. At the last king Henry the firste had pyte on them, and offered them thir own landes again and more, so that they would leave that place and go to Lamporte where he intendid to have a notable monasterie. But the monkes entretid him that they

might kepe theyr old house.' And so in the end they did. At Odcombe, a mile away, Thomas Coryatt, 'the Hierosolomytan- Syrian-Mesopotamian- Armenian- Median- Parthian-Persian- Indian- Legge-stretcher' hung up his travelled shoes in his father's church and said that the smoke of Odcombe was dearer to him than the fire of all other places under the sun; and the bells of Montacute church can be heard ringing in Kenya, in the home of a Montacute man who had a record made of them for love of his birth-place.

Beautiful things cluster round this hill of yellow stone. Brympton d'Evercy is near by, a Sleeping Beauty of a house, averting its 17th century garden-front as Rochester's lady shaded her lovely face; and the 12th century church of Stoke-sub-Hamdon, laid, in Leland's phrase, in the roots of the hill, has a most remarkable tympanum of Norman carving, and a smaller carving with one of the best dragons (a lean and active specimen) in the ranks of dragonry.

Further to the west, beyond South Petherton, is Barrington Court, another great Elizabethan house, full of pride and parade, with eupheistical pinnacles. Barrington is so much of its date that I have always thought of it as widowed, lacking inhabitants who could match it with an equal degree of unselfconscious arrogance. But one October afternoon I saw this amended. The house, just then, happened to be looking very pensive, for the failing light had washed its gold with silver and lengthened the severe perspective of the clipped yews and the central walk running between the raised lawns. A brown horse and a white pony were grazing in the paddock outside, and the gates between the garden and the paddock had been left open, so when the pony suddenly took it into her mind to stroll up the walk towards the house there was nothing to impede her. Presently her companion followed her. When he caught up with her he appeared to be remonstrating a little. She tossed her head, and stepped neatly up on to the left-hand lawn. He followed her, as Adam followed Eve, and together they strolled about the lawn, looking so exactly like the master and mistress of Barrington Court that if they had gone on towards the house and walked in I should have felt it to be perfectly natural and proper.

One of the charms of this tawny south Somerset stone is its great variability. Not only does it weather from its first butter-colour through every shade of golden tabby down to a greenish tint which is almost as dark as pond-water, but these hues respond like a chameleon to changes of light and humidity. I had never thought Crewkerne a town of much distinction (though it has a handsome large church with an acrostical epitaph in it, and a fair in late summer: it was at this fair in the innocent nineteen-twenties that I saw on a placard outside a booth the boastful claim: 'All Our French Artist's Models are Alive'); but one evening when the sun came suddenly out after a day of rain I saw Crewkerne light up with an intensity of colour I have never forgotten: topaz and beer-bottle brown, and tawny yellows beyond comparison.

From Crewkerne to Chard the road runs along the ridge of St Rayne's Hill and Windwhistle Hill, a watershed of regional landscapes, for to the south lies the rumple of west Dorset and to the north a very Somerset view of woodlands and sailing trees and the watery meadows of the Isle and the Parrett. South-eastward (I should have mentioned it before) lies the billowing country which half-hides the village of East Coker, added to English literature by a nomenclature of T. S. Eliot, and the Pendomer lanes where the primroses are so large and so plentiful, and an old golden-brown house couches blinking behind its yew trees, philosophic as an old tabby-cat who was a manor-house cat once and is now a farmhouse cat.

In the upper valley of the Isle is Ilminster, where Nicholas and Dorothy Wadham who founded Wadham College lie in the parish church under an altar tomb of preternatural length. Their manor house of Merrifield (of which Thomas Fuller says: 'His hospital

House was an *Inn* at *all times*, a *Court* at *Christmas*') stands a little to the north. I suppose the stretch of deserted canal near Merrifield and the further stretch by Hambridge are remains of the project for a canal running from the Devonshire coast to Bridgewater Bay. Even cared-for canals exercise what one might call a steadying influence on a landscape. These forsaken canals of the Isle valley deepen its prevailing air of sober unworldliness. They are like Sundays in a very quiet week. Sober unworldliness, too, seemed the characteristic of the old gentleman I once encountered, walking along the Ilminster-Honiton road with an umbrella in either hand. It was a fine day, he was perfectly in possession of his legs, he did not appear to be the sort of old gentleman who would carry two umbrellas for a wager, or snatch them up in an absence of mind. But he was walking towards Honiton, so perhaps he felt the Devonshire climate in the air.

Certainly, as one mounts into the Blackdown Hills one has the impression of having made a sudden jump westward. The fields become small and run at odd angles, assorting themselves to the fall of steep hillsides. Little heaths appear, patched in among belts of woodland, the views over gates show a more broken and tumultuous country, and there are at once fewer tokens of living and more lanes. Lanes in every degree of greenness and forsaken windingness branch off the roads, lanes which are rutted with cart-tracks, or closed off by sagging gates, lanes whose thick hedges grow out of stony banks, lanes that disappear downhill under green tunnels. If you follow them they will entangle you in further lanes, or take you, with an artful circumvention of contours, to some farmhouse perched halfway down a hillside, with a climbing field behind it dotted with sheep. I don't know why one should signalise houses, bridges, churches, and not lanes. In some landscapes, and this is one of them, a lane is the masterpiece. There is a lane turning off the Chard-Taunton road, a little before the old earth-worked headland of Castle Neroche, and running down to the valley of the river Ding (the Ordnance map will bear me out as to the name of this river) which for beech-trees and wild strawberries and a parachuting view can claim to be a masterpiece, even among the lanes of the Blackdown Hills.

A different kind of masterpiece, man having played a more intentional hand in it, is the colonnade of beech-trees on the road running westward towards the Wellington Monument. It is so prolonged, and the trees are so stately and so unanimous in growth and plait such an architectural vaulting overhead, that one becomes almost hallucinated by it, and looks out between the beech-bole columns with a sense that a different and much more out-of-doors world lies beyond them. It was here, at the foot of one of these beech-trees, that I found an impressive mushroom of the *cêpe* kind. Breaking it, I found that its blood-coloured hide covered a brilliant glow-worm green flesh, which from the instant of being exposed to air faded swiftly to a deadly slate-blue. So I was not much surprised to identify it in the *Petit Larousse* as *le Bolet de Satan, vénéneux*. But whether I should mention this mushroom is a delicate point, for I rather fancy it may have been growing in Devonshire, though I stepped from Somerset to pick it.

Wellington is very much in Somerset. It is one of the old clothing towns, and is still weaving. It lies snugly in the valley of the Tone, with a wide street and a sturdy well-cellared look about its Georgian houses (the fact that here a dark red brick varies the usual Somerset stone may have led me to choose the expression well-cellared). Its lamp-posts have hanging flower-baskets, a very pleasant custom; one likes to see a town with a nosegay in its button-hole. It also has a dead church. Dead churches are not uncommon in Latin countries, but one does not often see them in England. This one died comparatively young. To judge by its style, which could be described as chastened Gothic, it is not more than 150 years old. Far from chastened, and pretty wide of the mark of Gothic, is the entrance to the cemetery on the Tiverton road. Those who in childhood had a box of architectural bricks, made in Germany, and resented the fact that the bricks in the box never bore out the varied glories of the picture on the lid, can view this remarkable structure with a sense of fulfilment. This box really contained all the bricks.

Further west, between Milverton and Wiveliscombe, there is an example of a different outlook on burial. A signpost saying *Fry's Quaking House* points one up a lane. The lane is narrow as an eel, and at first it runs between banks that wear a thick sighing fleece of rough grass, and then it winds and tunnels among trees, and the sigh of grass is exchanged for the rustle and creak of branches. One needs sharp eyes to notice a couple of gateposts and a door, so old, so long disused, that they seem to be fusing into the bank. On the door, laced across by brambles, is an oval plaque with the words, *Friends' Burial Ground, 1681*. Inside the small enclosure there is only wild grass, bushes, trees (a dead one of great bulk and antiquity) and a few yews. In spring it must be full of birds' nests. I saw it on a silent day in August. The grass had seeded and was beginning to wither, and there were a few blooms of the pale purple wood betony. And that was all, except for a feeling of great wisdom and tranquillity.

Because we needs must hurry to the highest, and Exmoor is not so far distant, this unobtrusive pastoral county at the foot of the Brendon Hills has kept a particular seclusion and unvisitedness. Perhaps that is why Cothay Manor, in spite of its perfection as a specimen, seems a very natural dwelling-house, and its fifteenth-century wall-paintings, disclosed with the removal of generations of farm-house plaster and wall-paper, as entrancing, certainly, as reappearing violets and primroses in a spring-time wood, but not more surprising. A relic of its farm-house days that I remember seeing there was the massive wooden screw of an old cider-press — a Virgilian piece of craftsmanship.

I am back again at wood-carving: Milverton is another Somerset church with carved bench-ends (it has a tower, too). The Milverton bench-ends are full of spirit and accomplishment, and it seems to me that the faces of the Apostles are very Somerset faces. But the bench-end with the pestle and mortar on it is the best of all, both for design and that mysterious quality of statement. The carvings bring visitors to the church, and a visitor's book is provided for them, with a column for their remarks. Remarks do not, as a rule, spring readily from English visitors: *Wonderfully Peaceful*, or *Very Nice* are the usual sentiments. This made me the more awed by the Remark of a lady who dated the day of her coming *St. Matthias* and wrote: 'Art and Religion gloriously combined. Something missing on high Altar.'

At Wiveliscombe, further into the hills, there are more wood-carvings. But these are on the front of a house which has a Bank in it, and the house is hung with red tiles which do not make a very kind background to them. They are considerably more sophisticated than the Milverton carvings, and have a classical tartness which would make them very suitable as decorations to Donne's Elegies. Wiveliscombe was a weaving town, and had come to specialise in a coarse blue cloth called Penistones, which was bought by West Indian slave-owners for clothing their negroes. With the coming of Emancipation the owners expected to be ruined and the negroes expected to be made; but probably the most unequivocal result was felt in Wiveliscombe. No more penistones were bought for the West Indies, the cloth was too old-fashioned to find a market elsewhere, the manufactory too specialised to be made over to another weave. The looms were silenced. Such a calamity must have been felt all through the district, for cloth-making is an industry of many processes: dyeing, carding, spinning, fulling, tenting, shearing (the cloth, not the sheep), and involves such peripheral industries as teasel-growing, rack, card, and bobbin-making, and transport. To the older generation it was the end of a world,

as well as the end of a livelihood.

But the story of Wiveliscombe is only singular in its suddenness and compactness. Throughout the clothing districts of east and west Somerset the small fry wool centres were dwindling away, and there was not much else to turn to except farm-labour at eight or nine shillings a week. The drop in earnings may not have been so great, for the decaying industry paid bad wages too; but the drop in self-esteem must have been incalculable. Eve spinning had always held her head higher than Adam digging.

Bench-end, Crowcombe.

VI

THE QUANTOCKS
AND EXMOOR

*Where else should I be bore then in Tonton
Deane? ...*

Fuller, quoting this Somerset dictum, explains that: 'This is a parcel of Ground round about Tonton, very pleasant and populous (as containing so many Parishes); and so fruitful, to use their phrase with *Zun* and *Zoil* alone, that it needs no manuring at all. The peasantry therein are as *rude* as *rich;* and so highly conceited of their good Country (God make them worthy thereof!) that they conceive it a disparagement to be born in another place; as if it were eminently *all England.'*

The rustic self-sufficiency of the peasantry of Taunton Deane is also commemorated in that ballad about Young Urchard who courted the farmer's daughter with persuasions of ricks and sows, and when he could think of no more to say gave her a kiss and went away—all to the engaging refrain of doobicum-darbicum-doobicum-day. This ballad, of course, is no more a folk-song than I am. Some visiting London poet, like Sir John Suckling among the Wiltshire dairymaids, must have composed it, with a visitor's ear to the local dialect—like the Pepys party who 'called two or three little boys to us, and pleased ourselves with their manner of speech.'

A phonetic rendering of the Somerset manner of speech makes it look like the comic countryman. Actually it is a very pleasant dialect, and the habit of enveloping consonants in vowel sounds, which turns Richard into Urchard, Wookey in Ookey (Wells, by tradition, into Ools, but I have not had the fortune to hear this) gives it a caressing quality, like grace-notes. My first visit to Somerset was spent in a mattins and even-song devotion to an old man who drove cows past my door. His remarks to the cows were steadily injurious, but the tune of them was so persuasive and his voice so mellow, like a bass wood-pigeon, that the general effect was as edifying as a cello sonata. [22]

Taunton, whose growth has devoured so many acres of that earthy paradise of Fuller's day, is a nodal town. Roads and railways aim themselves at it from all directions and so too, less impetuously, does the Bridge-water-Taunton canal. To railway travellers Taunton is a place where there are quantities of trucks in sidings, and two church towers, either of which would be imposing enough to suffice any town except a wool-working one. To travellers by road it is a place with a great deal of outskirts, [23] though if the traveller comes from Langport he will not notice them much, for his mind will still be taken up with the ravishing views he will have had of West Sedgemoor. No town can be featureless which has a river running through it, and Taunton has its name-river, the Tone; but one can walk a long while without discovering it. There is a market-place of impressive width, and some of the smaller streets and alleys have a demure seed-cake sort of charm. But for the most part Taunton is an example of how dangerous it is for a town to have a great deal of room to expand in.

Taunton Deane, still a place good to be born in, lies under the shelter of the Quantock Hills. Here, if you pick up a handful of earth it feels resilient and unctuous, and when you let the handful drop it falls scattering and not as a clod. The contours of this good earth are gentle and ambling, and the fields have that peculiar appearance of being well-plumped-up (like eiderdown quilts) which characterises good tillage of the west-country small enclosure. It is a doobicum-darbicum landscape—and none the worse for that. If I were Minister of Agriculture I would collect all the popular writers and artists and travel-agency people together, and beg them to come down from their Wuthering Heights and great open spaces, and turn their powers of

A Church in the Quantocks.

description to celebrating verdant turnip-fields, dutch barns, and well-hung gates. Public opinion, in the end, gets everywhere; and a public opinion resenting expanses of subsidised thistles, mouldy ricks, and a slum density of half-starved cows to the acre would be a wholesome adjunct to English farming.

The air in this part of Somerset is as good as the soil; a soft yet lively air, like a light white wine. But even if I were not led by the nose to delight in Bishop's Lydeard I would still single it out as delightful. It lies turning its back on the main road, and looking towards the Quantocks, whose airy blue it responds to by being, itself, as full of varying shades of old rose-petal as a bowl of pot-pourri. Everything one has learned to expect of a church tower in this country of magnificent Perpendicular building is summed up in the tower of Bishop's Lydeard:

height, girth, progression from base to summit, ornament—all in such harmonious proportion that the total effect is of something immensely placid, a lion in contemplation. It is built of a warm vinous-red stone, and the stone's depth of colour makes it seem even more substantial. The same stone, of a later quarrying and more plum-coloured, appears in the village street, and gives it an appearance of sober gaiety; and on the hem of the village there is a rose-coloured manor-house, with a scalloping architecture which exactly conveys the pleasure of being rose-coloured.

Of all the profiles against the Somerset sky the profile of the Quantock Hills is the purest and stateliest. That is because Quantox or the Quantocks—as one says Mendip or the Mendips—is a narrow, straight-running range, and its narrowness allows it to achieve every inch of its height. Seen from the westward, where it rises most steeply, its outline is classical and severe. a statement of itself, as it were, a line of latin verse about a range of hills. Its eastern side has a more gradual fall. Seen from the level of West Sedgemoor it has a rounded and basking appearance, and the curves of a dolphin in an Italian decoration. The slopes are wooded, and moulded into combes and deep valleys. The summits are bare, with the elastic rise and fall of heathland. Even if one did not know, one would begin to think of people walking over those heights.

But of course one does know.

Most of us have had one year in our lives when everything happened at once and everything went amazingly; when all conversations were full of meaning, all projects feasible, all problems soluble, and each moon brighter than the last. This golden year usually befalls in one's twenties. Coleridge was twenty-five, Wordsworth twenty-seven, Dorothy Wordsworth twenty-six, when, on the thirteenth of November, 1797, 'he, my Sister and myself, started from Alfoxden, pretty late in the afternoon, with a view to visit Lenton and the valley of Stones near it; and as our united funds were very small we agreed to defray the expenses of the journey by writing a poem, to be sent to the New Monthly Magazine. Accordingly, we set off and proceeded along the Quantock Hills to Watchet, and in the course of this walk was planned the poem of "The Ancient Mariner".'

That is how things happen, in the year when everything happens at once. When Sara Coleridge spilled a kettleful of boiling water over her husband's foot just when 'some long-expected friends paid a visit to the Author's cottage,' S.T.C. sat at home and wrote *This Lime-Tree Bower my prison.*

They, meanwhile,
Friends whom I never more may meet again,
On springy heath, along the hill-top edge,
Wander in gladness and wind down, per-
chance,
To that still roaring dell, of which I told;

The roaring dell, o'er-wooded, narrow, deep,
And only speckled by the mid-day sun;
Where its slim trunk the ash from rock to
rock
Flings arching like a bridge—that branchless
ash,
Unsunned and damp, whose few poor yellow
leaves
Ne'er tremble in the gale, yet tremble still
Fanned by the waterfall. [24]

The friends (it was a poet's license which threw in that parenthesis about the possibility of never meeting them again, for they were certainly expected back to supper in the Author's cottage at Nether Stowey) were Charles Lamb and the two Wordworths. William and Dorothy immediately decided to settle within reach of Coleridge; and, for it was that fortunate year, almost as immediately found Alfoxden House to let, and rented it.

Even if this landscape of the seaward end of the Quantocks had been swallowed up by the sea or nineteenth century seaside resorting, it would still be one of the glories of the English scene, and we should know a great deal of it by heart. 'The flower-like woods, most lovely in decay,' the hidden brook *'That to the sleeping woods all night Singeth a quiet tune,'* Dorothy Wordsworth looking down from the silent winter hill-tops and seeing 'the villages marked out by beautiful beds of smoke.'

'Feb. 1st. The sun shone clear, but all at once a heavy blackness hung over the sea. The trees almost roared, and the ground seemed in motion with the multitude of dancing leaves, which made a rustling sound, distinct from that of the trees.

'Feb. 13th. Walked with Coleridge through the wood. The ridges of the hills fringed with wood, showing the sea through them like the white sky, and still beyond the dim horizon of the distant hills, hanging as it were in one undetermined line between sea and sky.'

Though the Alfoxden woods where Wordsworth 'used to take great delight in noticing

Bench-end, Trull.

the habits, tricks, and physiognomies of asses,' are emparked and assless now, Dorothy Wordsworth's *Journal* is still the truest guide to this landscape; a landscape, one might say, that matches her in sensibility; for its components of heath and sea and woodland sink into one's mind not so much for their natural beauty as for their aptitude to respond like an aeolian harp to the minutest changes of sky and mood of weather. 'In the footsteps of the poets' is a doubtful and hazardous itinerary; but one can follow it here, with one's mind full of Coleridge and Wordsworth and the Journal, and not feel oneself exiled by the century and a half which have gone by since these three young persons walked here together.

They did not, however, walk here very long. When the twelvemonth lease of Alfoxden ran out the owner's agent refused to let the Wordsworths renew it. He suspected them of holding Jacobin opinions. People living in the provinces are often remarkably intuitive.

Watchet, the first stage in the excursion which provoked *The Ancient Mariner,* was an appropriate destination, for it is both ancient and maritime. Twice sacked by the Danes, alarmed in mid-17th century by rumours of a Turkish pirate in the Severn Sea, Watchet, like Minehead and Porlock further along the coast, has a long history of fishing and sea-trading. More can come by sea than fish and lawful cargoes. These little West Somerset ports, so advantageously placed for trade with Ireland and Biscay, smuggled *de race* and almost, one might say, under license. This can be a bleak coast in late winter, when the north wind comes sharpened by the snow on the Welsh mountains, and local Justices of the Peace could scarcely be expected to keep warm by stag-hunting alone. Yet I have never heard that Cleeve Abbey is haunted—which is odd, since monuments of antiquity lying adjacent to smuggling routes usually mount a ghost or two to keep watch and ward over the barrels. Nothing is left of the Abbey church, but the living quarters remain, compact and functional as a last year's birds-nest. If one thinks of a last year's birds-nest as deserted, it becomes emotionally logical to cry into it, I suppose; and by dint of such words as forlorn or forsaken Cleeve can be made a melancholy place. It seems to me that Cleeve is much nearer to the qualities of dryness and detachment which one finds in the birds-nest and in Chinese poetry: a tranquil, hermitlike self-sufficiency.

During the civil wars Watchet saw a very remarkable action—I do not know whether to call it military or naval. Learning that a King's ship was standing off Watchet, loading a cargo, Captain Popham, for the Parliament, rode his troop of horses into the sea, surrounded the ship, and forced it to surrender. Dunster, further west, saw more serious fighting. Its Castle, 'everyway shut up with hills, except on the side which faces the sea,' was the last place in Somerset to hold out against the Parliament forces, surrendering on handsome terms after a five-month siege. Dunster Castle rises out of its woods with a fine air of rhodomontade, and rhodomontade is perhaps the word for its great oak staircase, carved with hunting-scenes and turbulent ornamentation. Dunster village has a celebrated yarn-market: a flourish of industry, as the staircase is a flourish of leisure. It is a beautiful example of practical elegance, an octagonal pavilion, set in the middle of the street so that buyers could approach it from all round, see the wares in a good light and yet do their trading under cover. Near by there is an old house whose front, hung with slates (practical too, in this rainy sea-bord climate) is a revelation of what the word *texture* can mean. In spite of being spitted on a main road and having a reputation among sight-seers, Dunster is unaffectedly old and quiet, and full of the sound and feeling of trees. On the hottest days of summer, when its streets are so drowsy and sheltered that one feels as though one were in the treacle well, along with Elsie and Tilly and Lacie, one hears the light to-and-fro of a fresher air brushing the wooded hillsides above it.

With this noise of trees in one's ears one looks back to the Quantocks, and knows them for what they: a boundary. West of the Quantocks, Somerset becomes a new county, at once rougher and richer. If one were an artist one would re-set one's palette, and choose new brushes with a shaggier stroke. If one were a musician, one would re-balance one's orchestra, charging it with horns and adding several bass-clarinets. To the writer, it is not so easy. I have said that it is rougher and richer, I am on the brink of saying that it is more romantic. Round the rougher rumples the richer romanticism ran —how many more Rs to express the fanfares of spring leafage in the Exe valley and the Horner Water? To the geologist everything is straightforward. His foot is now on the Devonian, and whether he towers over the whortleberry or the woods tower over him, he has only to be correct in order to be expressive (though even so he will find himself at the mercy of the Genius of the English Language, imposing its wild poetry into his Exmoor distinctions of Morte Slates and Hangman Grits, and finally tumbling him into Baggy Beds). This antithesis of the wood and the whortleberry, though, is really crucial. It is not that there are no more villages, manor-houses, churches, characters: there are plenty, and there is plenty one could say about them, and not very much that one can say about Exmoor. That is why Exmoor imposes itself, and insists on being attended to.

For the ordinary traveller there are two ways of approaching Exmoor from the east, that is to say, from Somerset. You can approach it suddenly, escalading it, as it were, from Dunster or Porlock. Or you can approach it *via* an anteroom, as one does dignitaries.

The escalading approach is the steeper and the more immediately dramatic. It gives one the pattern of the lanes that dive and burrow under the flanks of the moor, views that explode on the sight and are magicked away like smoke, the sense of almost violent seclusion in the hollow between the two heights of Exmoor and Bossington Hill, the woods that brim up the Horner Valley. As one climbs out of these woods and sees the bareness of the moor against the skyline one has a sensation of having been shot several hundred feet higher in a matter of moments.

For the anteroom approach one must begin further back, with the Brendon Hills. Structurally, the Brendons are the eastern flank of Exmoor, and judging them by a map one might think there was little justification for giving them a separate being, as if Somerset had not hills enough already. If they are a kind of cadet Exmoor, they have all the individuality of a younger brother, both in their steeply rounded sides, on which woods hang as romantically as Spanish cloaks, and in the mute brackeny heights above. The road from Elworthy to Wheddon Cross runs along the spine of the Brendons. It is a long patient uneventful road, and after some miles of it one gets a rather sinister impression of isolation, as though the villages of whose existence the downward lanes assure one were not really there, or were forsaken long ago, and that some crazy poet, and not a rural district council, had inscribed on sign-posts the lovely names of Huish Champflower and Withiel Florey. Villages do not die as easily as that; but for those whose taste leads them towards desolation the Brendons offer the unusual emotion of a Forsaken Railway, formerly used to carry the iron ore mined in these hills down to Watchet. And a very reproachful *sic transit* it is, with the fatalistic bankrupt kind of melancholy which only slighted usefulness can distil. It would be a wonderful place for a community of poltergeists to settle into, disillusioned poltergeists in search of a La Trappe.

In this anteroom approach to Exmoor there is no drama until the last moment, when between two rough stone gate-posts the untrammelled outline of Dunkery Beacon rears up before you. The sensation of having stumbled over the hind-quarters of a temporarily inattentive lion is one of the things to be urged for the anteroom approach. The other is, that if you continue northward over Dunkery Hill you will have your first sight of the Horner woods from above, whence they look so rounded, so voluminous, that you feel you could bounce on them, and that after a bounce or two they would toss you across to the woods under Selworthy Beacon.

Here you have the woods and the whortleberries, and the curious double rhythm set up between them, the curling triple measure of the woods, the slow spondees of the moor. Exmoor has no tors to accentuate it. Its contours rise and fall as soberly as the uncrested waves of mid-Atlantic. It is solemn, ponderous, and without rhetoric. But along the seaward edge the unrhetorical statement suddenly becomes eloquent with woods. It is as if the moor were brought to a halt by this richness of vegetation, and fell more steeply into the sea because of the woodlands weighing it

downwards. Here, after so many magnificently large and stately churches is Culbone— 'the smallest complete church in England,' [25] —lying in its narrow combe as neatly as if it were a nut which a squirrel had put away for the winter. It would be a hard nut to crack. Its walls are so thick that it seems quite as much massive as minute. This massiveness in small scale is typical. Exmoor cottages have chimneys like Suffolk Punches, and the old bridges, whiskered with ferns, look solid enough to carry an elephant though they are only wide enough for a pack-horse. Tarr Steps, a causeway of stepping stones across the river Barle, is another such piece of solidity. Being so unaccountably substantial and in so untravelled a place, they are said to have been built by the devil for his private use. [26]

It is not so much superstition as a creditable modesty which gives rise to these attributions. Superstition in its most weak-minded gullibility has spawned John Ridd's Farms and Lorna Doone's Dens up and down the Badgeworthy valley, and such quantities of excursionists are taken to Oare church to see the steps which were stained with the blood of a heroine who came out of the inkpot that it can only be a matter of a few years before bloodstains are plainly perceptible there. It pays some and hurts nobody is the excuse, I suppose. That excuse can hardly be urged for the other Exmoor Bunkum, stag-hunting. Unfortunately, hunting has acquired a mystical sanctity as a prerogative of those who can afford it. While they are ready to risk their horses' necks and their own in its defence these crusaders are not very likely to consider the sufferings of wild animals. Probably the best way to get rid of hunting would be to nationalise it, and make it possible for any one who wished to hunt to do so at a charge of sixpence.

The Barle and the Exe, that run to their waters-meet on the Devon border through such greensleeve valleys of hanging wood, both rise in Exmoor Forest, which in the matter of trees is no forest at all. This territory of heather and curlews and the soft dry moor-grass is at once sober and carefree. It has the seriousness of what is truly wild. I suppose its most affecting quality is its continuity, the way it goes on and on with scarcely a scribble of man's restless, defining, plotting and parcelling hand traced across it. Even the seasons have little power up here; the heather in bloom, the dead heather bells, answer the wind with the same dry whisper. But the long dusky undulations, the ridges hard as shoulder-blades, the soggy hollows prickled with rushes, are so allegiant to the weather that the movement of a cloud can transfigure them, and a breath of mist disembody them. Such a landscape is depersonalising. I remember getting out of a car to look for whortleberries, one August afternoon when the road across Dunkery Hill was lined with stationary cars, and the slope of the Beacon spattered with strollers and sitters. In a few minutes I was thinking of nothing but the pleasure of taking step after step, now feeling the crunch of moss underfoot, now treading on the short grass, now on the bared peat. The serious wildness of the moor had worked its spell on me, and swallowed me up. Thus walking inattentively in a circle I came back towards the road again. It was then that I noticed the faces of the people who had also got out of their cars to walk about on Exmoor for a little while. On every face I saw the expression which I knew my own face must be wearing: the expression of someone wandering in solitude and animal speechlessness.

Farm at Bawdrip in the Poldens.

VII
SEDGEMOOR

From the Quantocks and the Mendips, and the hills along the southern boundary, one is always looking down on some part of Sedgemoor, Sedgemoor so open to inspection and yet so mysterious and remote. Perhaps it is this quality of engagement with high ground, of washing the bases of peninsulas and promontories and lying in land-locked pools, which gives Sedgemoor its particular air of secrecy and import. It is like a green flood, whose very slow tide waxes to the greenest day in the year and then recedes to winter.

And even now I have not finished with the hills of Somerset. There are still the Poldens: a narrow range, running roughly parallel with the Mendips. They are small hills, but they do a great deal with their moderate resources, partly because of their characteristic bandings of exposed reddish stones; this, and being wooded, gives them a romantic Italianate look. I cast no slur on the Poldens when I say that they always strike me as a painted landscape, and that the Hood Column on the right-hand side of the road from Somerton to Street is placed just where it should be, with all the assurance of good scene-painting. But nature's hand added the smoky wreaths of Travellers' Joy, looping from the top of one hedgerow tree to another, which make this road so lovely through the flowerless months of January and February.

Somerton, the old capital of Somerset, lies at the southern end of the Poldens. It is a small, silvery town, with that very civilising feature, a town square, and a post-office whose wood-work is painted an unusual and becoming shade of petunia—the inn alongside is also trimmed with petunia, and between them they make a very agreeable group. The church has fine brass chandeliers, of a branching pattern common in Somerset churches, but these are further distinguished by their dedication 'To God's glory and the

On Sedgemoor.

honour of the Church of England 1782.' West of Somerton a spur of the Poldens runs to Langport, and on this spur is High Ham— a hill-top village with a certain Priddy-ish exclusiveness, and Low Ham, where the church stands in a bare field looking as mellow as a rick, and where the recent excavations of a Roman villa have uncovered a mosaic pavement illustrating the story of Dido and Æneas. There are remains of several Roman villas on the Poldens. Standing high, but not too high, these fertile slopes have just that golden mediocrity which a sensible Latin would appreciate.

These Polden Hills form a Sedgemoor watershed. To the east is the territory of the River Brue; to the west the territory of the River Parrett.

The Brue rises in the Wiltshire border, and begins to be a river in Parson Woodforde's country, flowing under large oak-trees and short thick bridges. The Cary accompanies the Brue in a sisterly way, keeping a course more to the south-west. A feminine river, shy, sly and gentle, the Cary imposes its ladylike character on a pastoral landscape of poplar screens dividing peculiarly slender fields, and wears like a family jewel the manor-house of Lytes Cary, with a garden full of clipped yew compartments, and a pair of very handsome gateposts rising from the scrambling margin of a country lane. The Cary's career as a river is not long. It has hardly slid through the Somerton Gap and begun to enjoy the pleasures of Somerton Moor before it is seized on—like any young woman seized on by matrimony—and disciplined into being the King's Sedgemoor Drain.

Keeping to the east of the Poldens, the Brue, embanked, and floored with water-lilies, traverses an expanse of very green flats, criss-crossed by lines of pollard-willows and draining ditches, towards Glastonbury. Here, I think, is the best on-the-level view of Glastonbury Tor; and I suppose it is the least seen, except by gipsies, who use these unfrequented roadsides for hanging out washing, whittling and bunching clothes-pegs, and boiling tea-kettles. But this is only

63

a forecast of the flatness and greenness of the Brue Level—'that fenny spacious tract', as Camden called it. Spacious is still the word Measured in miles it is not much, but its character is essentially spacious, and time seems to get oddly tangled into space, an hour here is much longer than an hour elsewhere. All the gestures of the landscape are slow; grazing cattle move through the pastures as majestically as barges; the man mending the ditch lifts another spadeful of black mud and deposits it on the bank as carefully as though it were a poultice; the water-rat gives an infinity of attention to his toilet; the tinman's van, with its bowls and saucepan lids reflecting the sun with a steady glare, has been drawn up for half-an-hour at the cottage gate. Even the policeman bicycling between the willow-banks is riding at a moderate speed.

Though draining and enclosure began here as far back as the 17th century, the pattern of the population is still pretty close to the pattern recorded in Domesday Book. The villages and hamlets stand warily dry-shod on small rises of ground. Both Meare and Pamborough are described by Domesday as islands: Pamborough a very Robinson Crusoe sort of island, for it consisted of six acres of ground, three arpents of vineyards, and one bordar; and was valued at four shillings. Wedmore is a handsome stone-built village with a pedigree. The treaty which Alfred made with the Danes after the victory of Ethandune was called the Peace of Wedmore, and in his will he bequeathed Wedmore to his son Edward. At Wedmore and in the neighbouring villages which string out along a small rise of ground there are such fine lilacs tossing over stone walls, such bright-coloured stocks and such flourishing ceanothuses, that it becomes possible to believe that a tolerable wine might have been made from the Pamborough vineyard. But they are only incidents in the spacious fenny tract, and winter puts them back in their place, with the sea-mist rolling in and the smell of earthy water blown over garden walls.

Even on the hottest and dryest day a sense of water washes round the fish-house at Meare. The Abbot of Glastonbury had a great fish-pond in the Brue Marshes, and the fish-keepers (as one says game-keepers) lived in this small stone house, with all their gear of nets and poles and osier baskets. Domesday records ten fisherman and three fisheries at Meare. This heron-grey Fish House, so sober and purposeful, is one of the most expressive mediaeval buildings in England. It now belongs to the best of owners, the National Trust. But I am not sure whether they ought to call it The Abbot's Fish House, which sounds misleadingly as though Abbots of Glastonbury came here for a little fishing. Abbots went hunting, but I very much doubt if they went fishing, for it was not until later that fishing as a sport developed from fishing as a labour.

Beyond Mark, where the church has a finely-panelled roof, Brue Level merges into Burnham Level, out of which Brent Knoll stands up as dominatingly as Glastonbury Tor, and even more astonishingly, since it rises from an unbroken flatness. Like Glastonbury, it is an outlier. Seen across the level it looks like a child's drawing, being so steep and so fortuitous; and even when you are close to it, it remains steep and surprising, the more so for being wooded in this sparse landscape of functional willow-banks. The spire of East Brent church is a seamark, and used to be kept white-washed to guide the ships in the Bristol Channel.

Along this stretch of the coast there is an odd territory of sand-dunes, spotted with bungalows and caravans, little huts and booths, all looking extremely uncomfortable and all expressing that steadfast British resolve to be happy and carefree at the seaside. It seems to have nothing to do with Somerset; and I would not be writing of it except for the accident that it was from the Brean and Berrow road, one rainy evening, that I looked inland and saw the Burnham Level, so undeniably green and yet one cannot forever be saying how green it is, washed with silver under a shining wet sky; and it looked so

37. Weston Zoyland church; an example of the Somerset timbered roof. *Crown Copyright*

38. Wedmore church, with its candelabras. *Sumner*

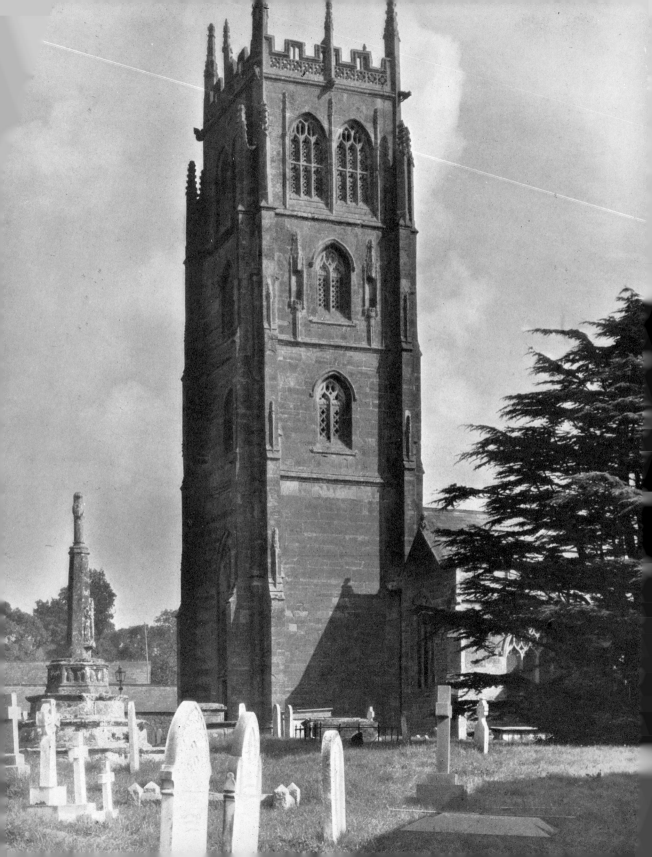

OPPOSITE

39. Church-tower and preaching
cross at Bishop's Lydeard.
Leonard & Marjorie Gayton

40. The zodiacal tympanum of the church-porch, Stoke-sub-
Hamdon. Sagittarius shooting at Leo.
A. F. Kersting

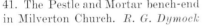

41. The Pestle and Mortar bench-end
in Milverton Church. *R. G. Dymock*

42. One of the wall-paintings uncovered at Cothay Manor.
Country Life

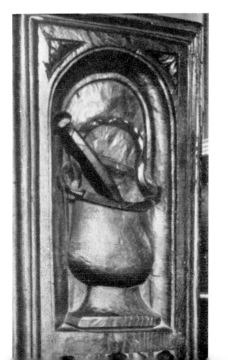

45. Ham Hill Quarry. The photograph shows the variability of the stone, which makes Ham stone buildings so animated.
Baynard Studios

OPPOSITE
43 & 44.
Cleeve Abbey.
Country Life

46. Montacute House, one of the garden pavilions. *Lloyd*

47. The eighteenth century brick-built Gazebo at Stowey Court. *A. F. Kersting*

49. Frozen fireworks. Detail of the roof-line of Barrington Court. *Country Life*

50. Montacute House, detail of west front. *Humphrey & Vera Joel*

48. Montacute House - 'high and disposedly,' like Queen Elizabeth's deportment when dancing. *Humphrey & Vera Joel*

51. Effigy in Montacute church. *Edwin Smith*

52. The Garden-
front at Brymp-
ton d'Everey,
late seventeenth
century.
Country Life

62. At Meare, in the Brue Level: the Abbot's Fish House. There is no abbatical significance in the upper window.   *Reece Winstone*

OPPOSITE

61. Straight ditches of all sizes, leaning willows of all ages, and plain-headed houses - the ingredients of a Sedgemoor landscape.
          Crown Copyright

63. Basket making from osiers on King's Sedgemoor.   *Crown Copyright*

64. Muchelney Abbey. *E. W. Tattersall*

65. Cloistered casks at Muchelney. *Country Life*

remote, so mysteriously sequestered, that I could not believe it would stay to be looked at longer than the time it takes to snap a soap-bubble.

The Brue and the Parrett run into the Bristol Channel not many miles apart, and share the Huntspill Level between them. They are both quiet, slow-running streams, and look as though their banks would not melt in their mouths. But the Parrett is the major river, richer in tributaries and, I think, richer in colour. Llewelyn Powys, writing with a native's affection and intimacy in his *Somerset Essays,* speaks of its 'modest cider-coloured reaches.' Some of that cider colour must be due to the same tincture of iron which colours Ham Hill stone, for the Parrett rises on the Somerset-Dorset border, and slides past the western shoulder of Hamdon Hill. Its first tributary is the Isle, and a little further on it is joined by the Yeo, another cider-coloured stream—and a full-bodied cider at that, having shuffled through much of the richest pasture land in Somerset.

It was in the valley of the Isle that a rather unusual country parson (he used to bless his parishioners' medicine bottles, which was believed to add considerably to the efficacy of what the doctor had put into them) heard his gardener break into a rambling ditty about sowing the seeds of love. The gardener was called John England. The parson was called Charles Marson. When Marson's friend, who was called Cecil Sharp, came to Hambridge to visit him, they began to collect old songs in the locality, and published the first volume of *Folk Songs from Somerset.*

The songs were plentiful enough, but gone under ground, for their singers were ashamed of such old-fashioned wares, while musicologists were remarking (often in German accents) that England, as distinct from Ireland, Scotland and Wales, had no music in its soul. [27] Like the battle of Waterloo, it was a damned near-run thing. If Marson had not been such an unusual parson that his parishioners did not mind what they sang to him, if he had not such a voluminous acquaintance among tramps, gipsies, and doddering old paupers, if the loosest woman in the neighbourhood had not carolled to him with as much confidence as if she had been a choir-boy in F, the incentive to other collectors of folk-songs might never have been given.

Folk-picture, alas, is a different story. No doubt we had it; but only very occasionally does an inn-sign or a rood-screen offer an English equivalent of those votive pictures which Samuel Butler so properly praised in *Alps and Sanctuaries.* The 17th century Apostles in Martock church are hard to assess because of their elevation and their concavity—they are painted into a series of niches high on the nave wall; but the King David who hangs about the north door is majestically vernacular, and so heartfelt, so tipsy with sweet psalmody, that to see him is to love his maker.

King David was the centre panel of a gallery, since pulled down, so in all probability paintings by the same hand flanked him. We must be grateful that somebody had the sense to preserve him, and hopeful that, since he was in the middle, he was the best of the bunch, like the rose in the middle of a country nosegay.

Martock church resembles an allegory of sacred and profane love. Its chancel is lean, even by 13th century standards. Its nave, for which the parish was responsible two centuries later, is so happy and glorious that it warms the heart to look at it. Its decorations flow over it, and the nobly brawny tower is finished off with a weather-cock which must be a friend to every child in the parish. The nave interior is as good. The timbered roof is superlative, even in this county of fine wood-work, and the stone screen which fills the western arch completes an effect of comfortable grandiosity. Cornet Richard Symonds who was here in 1644 noted that: 'The houses are built of a brave ffree stone, colour of umber, here growing. No gentleman lives in this parish, a low deepe rich grownde.' Martock is still a Ham Hill stone town, and there must be many houses which Richard Symonds saw, still in use; notably the old manor-house and the Court House; for the inscription on

81

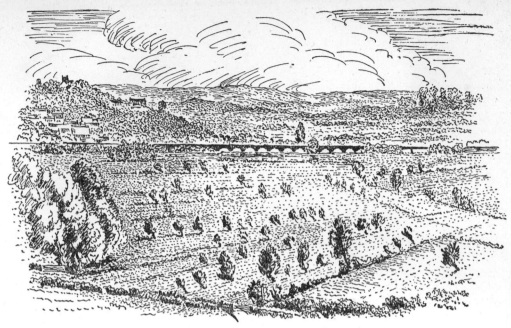

Sedgemoor near Langport.

it, 'Martock, neglect not thy opportunities' and the date of 1661, refer to its conversion to a grammar-school.

The Yeo comes into the county by cheese-making, glove-making Yeovil, and half-hoops a stretch of rather glum hedgerow country (famous for dairy-farming, however, and memorably sweet in summer dusks during hay-harvest). Ilchester, on the Fosse Way, midway in the course of the Yeo, is a queer squat town which looks as though it were matching itself to its horizons. It was a Roman town, and Roger Bacon was born here. In the 19th century it became infamous because of its jail. The outer walls of Ilchester Jail were so high that no sunlight reached the prisoners. The inner walls were 'wet as dung'—the simile of a country prisoner there. The governor, William Bridle, had been appointed on the strength of an apprenticeship to brutality in the hulks. He was dismissed, however, and the jail pulled down because of an account of the conditions, published by Henry Hunt

while he was a prisoner there. That is something which could not happen nowadays.

Beyond Ilchester the Yeo comes into one of those land-locked, fiordlike stretches of Sedgemoor, called King's Moor on the east of the Martock-Somerton road, Wet Moor (where the Yeo joins the Parrett) on the west. I remember seeing it from this road one winter's morning, when long rains had swollen it. Its lumbering speed and angry red-ochre colour made it a menacing sight. Already it was beginning to lap over its banks, and the water-logged moors were badged with pools and widening rivulets. When I came back later in the day the sky had cleared and was reflected in a brilliant expanse of floods, in which the Yeo was only perceptible as a thrust of water through water, like the movement of some furious shouldering fish.

The *ey* of Muchelney means *island*. Muchelney, Thorney, Middleney, are all names in this trident of Isle, Parrett and Yeo; and one sees the force of them when the floods are

Glastonbury Tor.

out. Muchelney has a beautiful old Priest's House, and the remains of a butter-coloured Abbey. The Abbey is now merged in a group of barns and ricks, a church tower looks over its shoulder, and smoke rises comfortably from the chimneys of the village. The technique of island life was different when the few serfs and bordars of Thorney and Middleney heard the Muchelney bells ringing across the swamp. A bishop who inspected Muchelney Abbey in the 14th century reported that the monks were infringing their rule by making themselves beds like tabernacles. An endless shiver of winter nights harps through the words.

It is strange to see the winter aspect of this landscape, which is dusky and rather severe, changed in a matter of hours to the vivacity of water. Floods, like snowfalls, by reversing the relative values of ground and sky convey a sense of levity. When one comes over the brow of a hill and finds trees standing up from a sky-blue surface instead of a sad-coloured one, it is impossible not to feel as if some delightful revolution had taken place during the night. This, of course, is followed by thoughts of all the people whose back-kitchens are flooded, whose cattle are endangered, whose autumn-sown onions may be washed out of the ground, who can't go shopping, etc. But except in very bad years, or where density of population has cramped the choice of building sites, floods are outwitted by management. Indeed, one might say that one has not seen Sedgemoor until the greater part of it is under water, for only then does one begin to appreciate its delicate economy of feet and inches above sea-level. Minute swells of ground never noticed before start up as islands and causeways, and the placing of houses and farm-buildings is seen to be as strategic as though they were demilunes and horn-works.

A good place from which to survey the floods is Langport churchyard. It lies on a neck of high ground, and one can look out as from the prow of a ship over sheets of water, speckled with island homesteads and trimmed with lines of willows and telegraph posts. Langport is a pleasant small town with steep streets and bridges and what is called a Hanging Chapel over the Huish Episcopi road—an enigmatical construction but very embellishing. Huish Episcopi has the loveliest of all the doctrinal Somerset church-towers, and a porch which matches it in spaciousness and serenity of design. The narrowed valley of the Parrett between the rise of ground by Curry Rivel and the steep wooded slopes by Aller is called the Langport Gap. There is a very fine view of the Gap from the Langport-Bridgewater road—a view which is a triumph of composition, for it has a little of everything in it, including a railway viaduct.

From Burton Pynsent near Curry Rivel (where the effigied Jennings tomb in the church includes some infant Jenningses done up in crimson sachets with only their faces showing) the elder Pitt, [28] walking among his plantations and hearing the masons at work on his column, must often have looked across West Sedgemoor, and the scalloping course of the river Tone, to Athelney—and as statesmen of his date were less officially modest than they are now, it may be that he sometimes made his own Plutarchian comparisons. It was to Athelney that Alfred the Great fled in that dire winter when England seemed lost. 'He forsook all his warriors and all his people, and crept by hedge and lane, through the wood and field, till he came to Athelney.' Afterwards he founded an Abbey in the place where he had found safety amid the floods and the reeds and the wet alder woods; and it was near Athelney that the Alfred Jewel was dug up: 'being plainly made,' says Camden, 'on purpose to hang on a string, it is very probable that he himself constantly wore it.' Later authorities prefer to think that he gave it to his Abbey.

Athelney is now merely the name of a little railway halt. The ruins on the skyline admired by railway travellers are those of a church begun and left unfinished in the early nineteenth century. But when the floods are out, and the osier plantations smoulder under water like an inlay of copper, and moisture lies on every undrowned object like a close grey fur, it becomes easy to imagine back to the winter of 878, to an Athelney which was England and to Alfred in his small kingdom biding his time as patiently as a heron.

Aelfred the Kinge, Engleonde's deorlinge, wrote the Saxon poet. Another England's darling haunts these watery lands, which were ruin to him as they were safety to Alfred. It is a story that when Monmouth was in Holland a fortune-teller said to him: *Beware of the Rhine:* which struck those who heard it as a rather unenterprising piece of prophecy. But rhine or rhyne is the name given to the great draining ditches which cut through Sedgemoor and hold it together. The Bussex Rhine, which halted Monmouth's men in their surprise attack on the royal forces, has been filled up. But one does not need to go far on Sedgemoor before finding oneself on the brink of one of these brimming ditches. Ten to one, like Monmouth's people, you do not know it is there until you are within a few yards of it. There it lies—muddy, nonchalant, unimpressive, and horribly disconcerting.

There is a vivacity of contradiction about a river which encourages the idea of getting across it. Rhines interpose themselves, which is a different thing altogether. Since the rhine is not to be crossed you walk along its margin. Presently you come to another wide ditch, which intersects the first. The landscape is as flat as a board, and you feel yourself pinned in your own square of it. Reason assures you that the fields could not be in use, that there could not be cows in one square and a haystack in another unless it were possible to move over the chess-board. But if you do not know the moves, and especially if it is foggy or dusky, the voice of reason can sound thinnish.

That is one mood of Sedgemoor. In another—equally unreasonable—the chess-board takes on an Alice Through the Looking-Glass quality of indefinite extensibility. 'Look,' says

Reason patiently. 'There are the Quantocks. Now turn your head and there are the Poldens. There is the tower of Othery, there is Middlezoy, there is Weston Zoyland. It is unusual to find three such fine churches lying so close to each other.' Meanwhile the part of you that doesn't listen to the voice of Reason persists in its belief that Sedgemoor is a limitless territory, and that Weston Zoyland tower only seems to be close because it is so tall. So you turn a deaf ear to Reason, and if you want to be further persuaded you lend yourself to the persuasion of the air. For of all things on Sedgemoor the most persuasive, the most personal to the place, is the air. It seems to have traversed a world-without-end of solitude, and all the smells it carries, the smell of the wild peppermint that grows along the ditches, the smell of a hay-stack, the bitter willow-scent, are qualified by water, just as the tone of stringed instruments is qualified by putting on a mute.

Other times, other smells. The road from Weston Zoyland to Bridgwater seems short enough to motorists. It seemed longer to those who rode or walked it in 1685, for gallows were set up all along it, where the rebels were left hanging and rotting in the harvest sun. The beautiful calm church of Weston Zoyland housed a sad congregation that July. An entry in the church register tells of 'about 500 prisoners brought into our Church, of which there was 79 wounded and: 5: of them died of thire wounds in our Church.' In the revolting story of the Suppression [29] it is reviving to find one upright man. Bishop Ken, accused of sedition, was asked if he had favoured the rebels and helped them when they were prisoners. He replied: 'It is well known in the diocese that I visited them night and day, and I thank God I supplied them with necessaries myself as far as I could, and encouraged others to do the same.'

Sturdy and plain-headed, Bridgwater is exactly the right town to stand in this mysterious and haunted territory. It clinches it by contradiction, as a bridge clinches a river. Bridgwater, the birthplace of Admiral Blake, has a most Protestant and most English air, and yet it could not conceivably be called prosaic, for the tide rushes through it, hammering the mud-banks of the Parrett estuary, and its sky is full of gulls, and its quays and riverside taverns have that indescribable maritime cosiness which no English person can behold without spiritual pride and sensual affection. Once a year this plain-headed town enjoys a glorious frenzy. Bridgwater Fair is one of the great Fairs of the West, especially in the matter of fireworks (a particularly unbridled form of squib is known as the Bridgwater Bullet). Beyond Bridgwater the estuary flows broadening on, past the Pawlett Hams where the grass is so rich that cattle can be fattened on this feed alone. Here the Parrett has been joined by the last of its tributaries, the Cary, *alias* the King's Sedgemoor Drain. With its full tale of tributaries, Isle, Yeo, Tone and Cary, and heavy with its compound of pastures and orchards and Sedgemoor flats and distant woodlands, it takes a last bend, and then flows due north into Bridgwater Bay.

I wrote at the beginning that I am unfitted by nature to compose a guide-book, and by now I must have made that clear. The things I have left out, Cheddar cheese and Exmoor ponies, towns, towers, mansions, and more British Earthworks than you would believe possible, are too numerous to be bunched up together in an apology. But one omission must be set right. I have said nothing of the melodious oddity of Somerset's place-names. Let them speak for themselves:

Cricket St Thomas, Cricket Malherbie, Binegar, Wanstrow, Norton Malreward, White Lackington, Chedzoy, Chilthorne Domer, Chilton Cantelo, Stogumber, Stogurzey, Babcary, Temple Cloud, Orchard Portman, Bason Bridge, Cradle Bridge, Queen's Camel, and Compton Dando.

NOTES

1 To judge by the quatrain on their wall tablet, Melancholy marked all the Burtons for her own.

Those who the longest life enjoy
Have told us with a sigh
That to be born seems little more
Than to begin to die.

2 Camden: *Britannia.*

3 *But lips that with deceit abound*
Can never prosper long;
God's righteous vengeance will confound
The proud blaspheming tongue.

Ps. xii. v. 3. N. V.

4 Camden: *Britannia.*

5 'Somerset is remarkable not only for its church-towers, but for the large proportion of ancient bells which they contain (mostly coeval with the towers), the total number being about 270, two or three counties in England only having more.' Victoria County History, *Somerset.*

6 Camden: *Britannia.*

7 Fuller: *Worthies of England.*

8 It seems likely that Sul does a little back-door magic to this day. On the eastern side of Solsbury Hill there is a long valley (with an Elizabethan house in it, called St Catherine's Court.) A friend of mine, walking in this valley, stopped to talk with a woman, and commented on the spring beside her cottage. 'It is good for the eyes' she was told. 'My mother always kept a bottle by her, and they say it is because the spring faces sunrise on Midsummer Day.' Another venerable character, the ithyphallic Giant of Cerne Abbas, was, within living memory, resorted to by childless couples, who took him gifts of eggs. How can our bishops say that England is no longer a religious country?

9 Celia Fiennes gives a very full account of the ceremonial of bathing (c. 1687) including the 'garments made of a fine yellow canvas, which is stiff and made large with great sleeves like a parsons gown, the water fills up so that its borne off that your shape is not seen' and the 'broad brim'd hatt with the crown cut out' worn by those being 'pumpt on their heads for palsyes.'

10 The Baedecker air-raid on Bath puts this sentence into the past tense.

11 Memoirs of Harriett Wilson.

12 The Somerset coal-field was the last to abandon the custom of using boys in harness as haulage-animals.

13 Bath. Illustrated Guide Book Series. Ward, Lock & Co.

14 The Miner's Arms has recently changed its name, more's the pity.

15 'A Cistern allwayes full of water, it looks cleer to the bottom which is all full of stones as is the sides, just like candy,' is the description given by Celia Fiennes, who was shown round by candlelight in 1698.

16 Victoria County History.

17 Somerset has two Yeos, this one, and the Yeo which runs through Ilchester.

18 The local industry was mining and calcining calamine ore, the latter being both thirst-provoking and subject to spells of unemployment.

19 Somerset churches have escaped the worst furies of purification, restoration, and embellishment—perhaps because it became a backward agricultural county at the time when These Three were at their busiest. One of the most fortunate survivals is at Croscombe, near Wells, where the church has its Laudian fittings. Perhaps the most flawless period specimen is Corton in south-east Somerset. Old Corton church having become ruinous was entirely made over in 1869. The interior is the purest Kilvert. It is already a fascinating document, and provided no one gets prim about it in another fifty years it will be an ecclesiological treasure.

20 'Four gallons a day per man used to be the harvest allowance in Somerset when I was a boy.' This is George Saintsbury, writing his *Notes on a Cellar-Book*, and remembering the 1850s.

21 Other fine barns are at Wells, Glastonbury English Combe, and West Pennard.

22 One reason for the euphony of Somerset speech is the substitution of Z for S. The sharp S has a much higher vibration frequency than any other consonant. One has only to compare the moral overtones of *hissed* with *hizzed* to understand why a speech which blunts the sharp S sounds kindly. I remember being told by Sir Richard Paget, that great explorer into the mechanism of speech, that in the early stages of broadcasting the sharp S was so unsettling to the microphone that a modified Somerset version had to be used by broadcasters. I remember, too, another tribute to the melodious quality of Somerset speaking. In a pre-sound-track film of the twenties where the cooing of a dove was called for, the dove was a Somerset man.

23 Outskirts relieved by a very graceful and distinguished group of new houses on the Ilminster road. The round-headed doorways in the connecting walls have a Kate Greenaway look which seems particularly suitable to a country-town building scheme.

24 Here is Wordsworth, forty years later, recalling the same scene. 'Across the brook had fallen a tree, an ash if I rightly remember, from which rose perpendicularly, boughs in search of the light intercepted by the deep shade above. The boughs bore leaves of green that for want of sunshine had faded into almost lilywhite; and from the underside of this natural sylvan bridge depended long and beautiful tresses of ivy which waved gently in the breeze that might poetically speaking be called the breath of the waterfall. This motion varied of course in proportion to the power of the brook.'

25 Cox and Ford, *Parish Churches of England.*

26 I should mention another Somerset work by this Master: the Wansdyke, an earthwork running from Clevedon to Inkpen Beacon. He named it Wansdyke because he built on on a Wednesday.

27 Marson himself had lived for eight years in Somerset without suspecting the existence of a Somerset folk-song.

28 If so many little Jenningses had not been laid away in sachets Pitt would not have been there. William Pynsent, who left him the property, got it through marrying a Jennings heiress.

29 Jeffreys was only more showly vile than the rest of the King's party. Mary of Modena, that virtuous queen-consort, complained furiously at being allotted only 98 Somerset prisoners to make her profit on by selling them as slaves to the Virginia plantations, and demanded 100 more.

INDEX

Italics refer to photograph numbers